Desmond Rainey is a retired civil servant, having worked in the Department of Agriculture and Rural Development for over 40 years. He is an elder in 2nd Comber Presbyterian Church, and has in the past sung in the church choir, participated in amateur dramatics, and played badminton and tennis. He has always been fascinated by history and was a founder member of Comber Historical Society. Desmond is also an avid collector of old postcards, photographs of Comber and music of the 1960s. He is co-author of *A Taste of Old Comber*.

Laura Spence is a producer in BBC Northern Ireland mainly working on history and local interest documentaries. Recent projects include *A Narrow Sea* – a 60 part series tracing the connection between Scotland and Ireland; and *Hidden History*, an ongoing radio series which travels Ulster's highways and byways, 'rolling back time'. Laura is a committee member of Comber Historical Society and has a passion for history and genealogy. In her spare time, she works with animals from Assisi Sanctuary.

Thomas Andrews, second from right,
with other Harland and Wolff apprentices (1889)

A World Record. One third of a mile of iron and steel in two ships.
The White Star Liners *Olympic* and *Titanic* at Belfast. The ill-fated *Titanic*
(to the right), lost with 1,500 souls, April 15th, 1912

A Chronicle
of Comber

The Town *of*
Thomas Andrews

SHIPBUILDER
1873–1912

DESMOND RAINEY
AND
LAURA SPENCE

ULSTER HISTORICAL FOUNDATION

To our parents

This publication has received financial assistance
from Ards Borough Council.

Ulster Historical Foundation is also pleased to
acknowledge support given by the individual
donors and subscribers. All contributions have
made this publication possible.

COVER DESIGN BY DUNBAR DESIGN
Image of Thomas Andrews courtesy of Belfast Harbour

First published 2011
by Ulster Historical Foundation,
49 Malone Road, Belfast BT9 6RY
www.ancestryireland.com
www.booksireland.org.uk

Printed by Martins the Printers
Design by FPM Publishing

Contents

Foreword

I am honoured to be asked to write this foreword for Desmond Rainey and Laura Spence's wonderful book which contains so much history and interesting information. They have carried out a vast amount of research on Comber at this particular period, adding to that done in the past by the late Norman Nevin. Much of the content is new to me.

The book portrays the story of Comber during the lifetime of my great uncle, Thomas Andrews Junior who was chief designer at the shipyard of Harland and Wolff during the construction of *RMS Titanic*. Indeed many Comber people helped build the mighty ocean liner. Unfortunately Uncle Tommie lost his life when the ship sank in 1912. So many lives lost – it was such a tragedy and was not often spoken about, either in my family circle or in Belfast. Harland and Wolff reckoned it was a bad advertisement for the shipyard and tried to have films and a play about *Titanic* banned. Nowadays things are different.

But this book is not primarily about *Titanic*. It tells of life in a little Co. Down town at a period when it had industries such as the flax spinning mill and the distilleries producing the famous Old Comber Whiskey, a town well known for cricket and for Sir Robert Rollo Gillespie. It is a town in which I grew up, spending many happy years working in the mill, which is now unfortunately closed. This book is largely about people and over the years I have come to know many Comber people. It was no different in the days of my grandfather and great-grandfather. They were all part of the community, and it was into this community that Thomas was born in 1873. This book traces the story of those Comber people throughout Thomas' lifetime, and it is interesting to think that the stories contained in these pages, gleaned from old newspaper reports, would have been known to Thomas.

The story of Thomas Andrews and Titanic holds a timeless fascination. So does the story of Comber. I wish Desmond and Laura every success with this new book.

J.M.J. ANDREWS

Introduction and Acknowledgements

On 31 May 1911, huge crowds gathered at the Thompson Dock in Belfast to watch the largest ship in the world glide from her slipway into the River Lagan. Just under a year later even greater numbers of people listened in shock to the news that *RMS Titanic* had sunk with the loss of 1,500 lives.

Nowhere was the news more heartbreaking than in Ulster: in Belfast where the great ship was conceptualised, planned, built and launched; and in Comber, County Down, home of the ship's designer, Thomas Andrews Junior, who drowned that April night in 1912 at the age of 39.

One hundred years on, the world is still fascinated by the tragic story of *RMS Titanic* and those who sailed on her. However, while the name of Thomas Andrews Junior is well-known, it is in the little town of Comber that he is best remembered – the town where his family still live today. Ardara, the home of his childhood years, still stands, while the North Down Club, of which he was a member, continues to dominate Ulster cricket. At the Non-Subscribing Presbyterian church where he worshipped you can see Thomas' name inscribed on the headstone of the family grave. You will also find in the town a magnificent memorial hall, which stands as a lasting tribute to one of Comber's best loved sons.

Comber, during Thomas Andrews' lifetime, was an industrious mill village, shaped by the 'gentry' who drove its linen enterprise – the Andrews family. As we mark the centenary of the loss of *Titanic* in 2012, this book looks back to that time – to the town that Thomas would have known, to his family and the people who were his neighbours; the organisations and clubs he would have attended; the issues of the day which would have provided mealtime conversation round the dining table at Ardara. This is the story of a small town, a big family, a huge ship and an immeasurable loss …

The authors wish to gratefully acknowledge the following people whose support has made this publication possible:

Kathleen Coulter and the committee of Comber Historical Society
Len Ball
Erskine Willis

Kim Cleland
The Andrews family, especially John, Tom and Johnny
Diane Taggart
Rev. Ian and Mrs Sandra Gilpin
Ian Shields and North Down Cricket Club
Newtownards Chronicle
The Public Record Office of Northern Ireland (PRONI)
The Newspaper Library at Belfast Central Library

Finally, a big thank you to Fintan Mullan, Executive Director of Ulster Historical Foundation, and his team of workers for their guidance in the publication of this book, and to all those patrons and subscribers who contributed to the costs of production.

DESMOND RAINEY AND LAURA SPENCE

Donors and Subscribers

The authors and publisher would like to thank the following donors and subscribers whose generosity has helped to make this publication possible. All contributions are gratefully acknowledged.

Ards Borough Council
Sam and Helen Long
Mr Desmond Rainey
Mr and Mrs E. Rainey
Mr D.E. Willis

Mr Len Ball
Comber and District Horticultural Society
Comber Historical Society
Alan Dunlop
Mr Joe Johnston
Mr Hugh A. McWhinney
Rotary Club of Comber

Mark Anderson
Anonymous
Mrs Nessie Beers
Kim Cleland
Kathleen Coulter
Trevor Cummings
Cindy Douglas
Alison Finch
Georgian House Restaurant
Winifred Glover Insurance
Adrian and Marion Hanna
David Huddleston

Loughries Historical Society
John and Donna McBride
Johnnie and Netta McBride
Sam McIlveen
Martin and Marianne Perry
Roy and Katy Spence
Cecil and Muriel Stevenson
William Suitor
Robin Thompson
Brian and Jean Tompsett
Irene Watterson
Alf and Elizabeth Whitehead

Painting of Comber, 19th century

1
1912 – Disaster on the High Seas

The year 1912 will be remembered for many things. There was war in the Balkans. Woodrow Wilson was elected as US President. Captain Robert Scott and his companions perished on their return from the South Pole, having been pipped at the post by the Norwegian Roald Amundsen. And in Ulster a Covenant was signed by thousands of Unionists opposed to Home Rule by a Dublin parliament. But one event stands out above all others, an event ingrained in the global memory, and that event concerns a ship – the mighty *Titanic*.

RMS Titanic, of the White Star Line, was a Belfast ship, built in the shipyard of Harland and Wolff. She was launched on 31 May 1911, and left Belfast for Southampton on 2 April 1912. From there she was bound for New

RMS Titanic – last farewell to Belfast

Thomas Andrews Junior, 1873–1912

York, on her maiden voyage across the Atlantic. Belfast was justifiably proud of *Titanic*, the largest ship in the world, a ship that was unsinkable. Yet tragically this unsinkable ship sank. What went wrong?

Titanic set sail from Southampton on 10 April 1912 under the command of Captain Edward John Smith. She called at Cherbourg in France and then at Queenstown (now Cobh) in the south of Ireland. From there it was open sea all the way to New York – and icebergs. Some of these were the size of small mountains, and it was *Titanic*'s misfortune to collide with one of these off the coast of Newfoundland on the night of 14 April. The iceberg struck below the waterline on the starboard side, and water flooded into the boiler rooms through a 300 foot gash in the hull.

At first most people on board were blissfully unaware of what had happened. There was a slight bump, but that was all. However, within two and a half hours *Titanic* was no more. It had sunk to the bottom of the Atlantic, lights still blazing, the band playing, hundreds of passengers and crew struggling in the water. All too few made it on to the lifeboats and eventual rescue by ships such as the *Carpathia*. Out of a total of 2,201 souls on board, there were only 712 survivors. One man who perished was Thomas Andrews of Comber, County Down, the designer of the ship.

Thomas Andrews was a hero during the final hours. The following cablegram was dispatched by the White Star Line from its New York Office:

> After accident Andrews ascertained damage, advised passengers put heavy clothing, prepare leave vessel. Many sceptical about seriousness damage, but impressed by Andrews' knowledge, personality, followed his advice, saved their lives. He assisted many women, children to lifeboats. When last seen, officers say was throwing overboard deck chairs, other objects, to people in water. His chief concern safety of everyone but himself.

One survivor, a Mr Dick, had this to say:

We begged him not to go [down below to investigate], but he insisted, saying that he knew the ship as no one else did and might be able to allay the fears of the passengers. When he came back we hung on his words. They were these: – 'There is no cause for any excitement. All of you get what you can in the way of clothes and come on deck as soon as you can. She is torn to bits below, but will not sink if the after bulkheads hold. She has been ripped by an underlying peak of ice, and it has torn away many of the forward plates and bolts'. He knew that he would lose his life, and yet he behaved so nobly that his heroism is worthy of the greatest praise, as he certainly knew the danger we were in, yet voluntarily sacrificed his life.

Titanic founders with the loss of 1,500 souls

Comber and its hinterland, from an old map *c.* 1900

2

Comber in Shock

This is how the *Belfast and Province of Ulster Directory* of 1912 describes the home town of Thomas Andrews:

> Comber is a market town in County Down, fourteen miles from Downpatrick, seven E.S.E. from Belfast, situated on the road from Belfast to Downpatrick. There is a large square, where fairs and markets are held, and in the centre of which stands a handsome Masonic monument, erected to the memory of General Gillespie. The River Comber, upon whose banks the town is situated, and from which its name is derived, runs into Strangford Lough, on the east side of the parish, and the tide flows to within a short distance of the town. There are two extensive distilleries, corn mills, hotels, a bleachgreen, a spinning mill, and stitching factory. The Church of Ireland is a neat little building. There are places of worship for Presbyterians, Unitarians, Methodists, and a Roman Catholic Chapel. The educational institutions are a school, founded by Viscountess Castlereagh in 1813, one under Erasmus Smith's Charity, and Congregational and National Schools. A National School is attached to the Second Presbyterian Church, called Smith's National School. There are two Masonic Halls and an Orange Hall. The North Down Cricket Club has been in existence for over half a century, and still maintains its old prestige. There are also hockey and football clubs. The market is held every Tuesday. Fairs – January 5th, April 5th, June 28th, and October 19th. The population in 1911 was 2,589.

That little town was now plunged into mourning for Thomas Andrews. The townsfolk joined in the grief of the Andrews family, with memorial services being held in all the Comber churches. At the Non-Subscribing Presbyterian Church in Comber, where the Andrews family worshipped, Rev. Thomas Dunkerley had some very moving words to say at an emotionally-charged morning service on Sunday 21 April, taking as his text the words of John 15:13 – 'Greater love hath no man than this, that a man lay down his life for his friend'.

Rev. Thomas Dunkerley

Thomas Andrews had been a personal friend, and Rev. Dunkerley delved back into his boyhood, remembering two inseparable brothers growing up in the congregation and passing through his communicant class – Thomas and John Miller Andrews (later to be Prime Minister of Northern Ireland). He mentioned in particular an incident at a church bazaar held in 1879 when a number of kittens were to be offered for sale. One escaped, and it was the 6-year old Thomas who persuaded the frightened creature to abandon its place of refuge, inaccessible to humans. As a result he was allowed to keep it. The animal recognised where it could place its trust, and the Rev. Dunkerley illustrated how trifling incidents such as this showed indications of Thomas' character, even at an early age. He emphasised the many qualities of Thomas – intelligent, industrious, earnest and enterprising, whose work must be good and true, satisfying his own exacting conscience. When he heard that *Titanic* had been lost, Rev. Dunkerley shared his reaction with the congregation; he just knew that Thomas had gone down with the ship because it was not in his nature to save his own life at the cost of that of others. And indeed this had been borne out by tales relayed from the stricken liner of his heroism to the last. Rev. Dunkerley asked for 'blessings on his memory', and finished by saying 'And it may be that he, beholding us, blesses us'.

At the close of the service a resolution of sympathy with the family was passed at a congregational meeting, and a similar resolution was drawn up by all the Comber ministers. Sentiments of condolence were expressed by many individuals and bodies in the town such as North Down Cricket and Hockey Club. A copy of Rev. Dunkerley's sermon can be found in Appendix 1.

3

The Andrews Family of Comber

Sir Robert Rollo Gillespie stands guard over Comber Square *c.* 1900

Let us roll back the years to 1870. In that year, as indeed today, the most obvious reminder of Comber's history was to be found in its Georgian Square – the monument to Sir Robert Rollo Gillespie. Many are the tales to be told of Rollo, but this book is not primarily concerned with him. Suffice it to say that he was born in a house in Comber Square in 1766, and became a famous soldier rising to the rank of Major-General in the armies of George III. He fought against the French and their allies in the West Indies, later in India and Indonesia, and finally went to meet his Maker after being struck down outside the fortress of Kalunga in Nepal in 1814. Allegedly, he is said to have exclaimed in his final moments, 'One shot more for the honour of Down'.

The main object of our interest is with the Andrews family, and on 15th September 1870 the Rev. John Orr of Comber Non-Subscribing Presbyterian Church conducted a wedding there. The happy couple were Thomas Andrews of Comber and Eliza Pirrie. This is how it was announced in the *Belfast Newsletter* of the following day.

MARRIAGES.

ANDREWS—PIRRIE—September 15, at Comber, by the Rev. John Orr, Thomas Andrews, to Lizzie, daughter of the late James Pirrie, Quebec.

The groom would later become known as Thomas of Ardara, because he took up residence in Ardara House on the Ballygowan Road in 1871 (he greatly extended it in 1904). He had been born in 1843, the youngest of three brothers who were directors of the Comber flax spinning mill of John Andrews & Co, the others being James and John. A fourth brother, William Drennan, had gone into the legal profession and was living in Dublin. There was also a sister Frances, still unmarried in 1870.

These were the surviving children of John Andrews, whose dream the spinning mill had been. Alas, he never lived to see it in operation, for he died just a few weeks before its opening in 1864. This John had taken an active part in public affairs, eventually serving as High Sheriff of County Down in 1857. He was also land agent for Lord Londonderry, who owned much of Comber, from 1830.

Thomas Andrews 1843–1916, father of the shipbuilder

But it was Thomas of Ardara himself who had personally supervised the building of the mill at the early age of 20, and all without the use of a contractor. He was described as 'plodding and persevering by nature'. As we shall see, there was a brilliant future ahead of him, and he would father a remarkable family.

In 1870 the mill was a major employer in Comber, producing high quality yarn which was woven into linen cloth elsewhere. It gave work to over 500 people and was an impressive monument to the enterprise of the Andrews family. But it was not the only one. For the imprint of the Andrews family was deeply embedded in the physical environs of the town.

Comber was a hubbub of activity. For apart from the spinning mill, there were two distilleries manufacturing the renowned Old Comber Whiskey, although the Andrews family had not been involved in this business since 1788. But they were involved in just about everything else. In 1870 the three brothers were also partners in the firm of James Andrews & Sons, along with

Comber Flour Mill. Note the grain store of 1863 in the right background

two uncles, William Glenny and Isaac, and their cousins (Isaac's sons) Thomas James and John – although John was working in Liverpool at this time, and did not return to take an active part in the Comber business until 1876. There were various strands to this business.

There was flour-milling, carried on in an impressive 5-storey flour mill, built in 1771. The entrance was down Mill Lane, opposite where is now Rosie Scott's pub. Allied to this was another large building, the grain store of 1863. This was eventually demolished in 1978 following a fire started by vandals. And there were corn mills at Laureldale (known as the Upper Mill, close to where Comber Christian Centre is today) and on the banks of the River Enler (the Old Mill). But there was to be no long-term future for flour-milling in Comber. By 1879 the firm of James Andrews & Sons would be dissolved, leaving the flour milling side of the business in the hands of Isaac and his sons. The new firm of Isaac Andrews & Sons moved to Belfast in 1883, shortly after Isaac himself had died.

There was also a linen wash mill and bleach green where large pieces of cloth would be left out in the open air to whiten. And there was a beetling mill which had been in existence since about 1762. Beetling was a process whereby heavy pieces of timber rose and fell on the linen, putting a finish on its surface and thus adding value. But by 1870 the bleach green was in difficulties – out of date and losing money. It was to close in 1872, and later became famous as the ground of the phenomenally successful North Down Cricket Club, which was to

John Andrews the Great
1721–1808

The Mausoleum built by William Glenny Andrews

chalk up numerous victories in the Ulster Senior League and Cup competitions. In 1870 the Andrews family were already heavily involved in the affairs of the Club, which had been formed in 1857.

Much of Comber's industrial enterprise had been the brainchild of Thomas of Ardara's great grandfather, another John, sometimes called John the Great because in the 18th century he transformed Comber from what Walter Harris somewhat unfairly called 'a mean little village' into a real hive of industrial activity. When he died in 1808, his youngest son James took over. James had the entire industrial complex re-organised and modernised during the 1830s, introducing a steam engine to pump water to the flour mill and bleach green, erecting new water wheels and constructing the spring dam. He was also a founder and benefactor of the Non-Subscribing Presbyterian Church, and donated land on which a meeting house was built in 1838. James died in 1841.

Let us take a wander down to St Mary's Parish Church, built in a corner of the Square in 1840 on the site of that of the 17th century Scots settlers. Indeed this has been an ecclesiastical site from medieval times, when there was a monastery here, but all trace of this has long since gone. Just three years previously, in 1867, William Glenny Andrews, an uncle of the bridegroom, had erected a large mausoleum, appropriately decorated with funerary urns, in the churchyard of St Mary's. We can guess from this magnificent

IN THE VAULT BENEATH REST THE MORTAL REMAINS OF

THOMAS ANDREWS

BORN A.D. 1698. DIED A.D. 1744.

AND ALONG WITH OTHERS OF HIS FAMILY

HIS SON JOHN ANDREWS

BORN A.D. 1721 DIED A.D. 1808

WHO HELD A COMMISSION IN THE DOWN MILITIA IN OPPOSING THE LANDING OF THE FRENCH
IN IRELAND IN 1760 AND WAS THE CAPTAIN OF A COMPANY OF THE VOLUNTEERS IN 1779-82
RAISED AT HIS OWN EXPENSE IN WHICH HIS SON JAMES ANDREWS AND SEVERAL OF HIS OTHER
SONS WERE LIEUTENANTS.

HE ERECTED THE TOMB WHICH IS BENEATH IN 1788 IN WHICH REST THE
MORTAL REMAINS OF HIS WIFE MARY ANDREWS (CORBIT) AND SEVERAL MEMBERS OF THE FAMILY

"BLESSED ARE THE DEAD WHO DIE IN THE LORD"

THE REMAINS OF THE FOLLOWING ALSO REST IN THE VAULT BENEATH

SARAH ANDREWS.

BORN 12TH NOVEMBER 1827 DIED 17TH OCTOBER 1829

SARAH ANDREWS

BORN 23RD MAY 1834. DIED 2ND MARCH 1845

MARY ANN ANDREWS (DREW)

BORN 22ND AUGUST 1822 DIED 5TH APRIL 1852.

MARY JANE ANDREWS (JEFFERY)

BORN 13TH OCTOBER 1847 DIED 17TH MARCH 1879.

JAMES ANDREWS J.P.

BORN 23RD NOVEMBER 1829. DIED 7TH FEBRUARY 1882.

JANE ANDREWS (QUINN)

BORN DIED 4TH OCTOBER 1882

MARY ANNE ANDREWS.

BORN 29TH JULY 1869. DIED 25TH FEBRUARY 1885

AMY ANDREWS.

BORN 2ND AUGUST 1865 DIED 20TH FEBRUARY 1894

SARAH ANDREWS (DRENNAN)

BORN 10TH APRIL 1807 DIED 13TH FEBRUARY 1902.

JOHN ANDREWS J.P.

BORN 27TH JANUARY 1838 DIED 28TH MARCH 1903.

Marble tablet on Mausoleum

monument that we are in the presence of a family who have played a
significant role in Comber's history. There are no burials inside the
mausoleum, but it is built over the family tomb, and plaques on the walls
detail those who lie interred beneath.

Uraghmore, one of only two three-storey houses in the Comber of the 1830s

The earliest name recorded is that of Thomas (born 1698). He was probably the descendant of settlers who had come over from Scotland in the time of James Hamilton and Hugh Montgomery, and we find a Thomas and Robert Andrew mentioned in the 1630 Muster Roll for Mahee as tenants of Viscount Claneboye (James Hamilton). It was Thomas who established the family's interest in milling back in 1722 when we find him working the Upper Corn Mill at Laureldale. He also made soap and candles, a business which ceased in 1788. But by then Thomas was dead, having passed away in 1743 at the early age of 45.

Other names already mentioned had also found their last resting place here. In 1870 here were the remains of Thomas' son, John the Great (1721–1808), of James (1762–1841) and of John (1792–1864), the father of Thomas of Ardara.

The original house of John Andrews the Great had been built in 1744 in Castle Street, where Supervalu is now sited. From 1792 it had been called the Old House, because in that year a new house was built opposite for John's son James when he married Frances Glenny. They called their house Uraghmore, the place of the big yew trees, after ancient trees in their garden believed to be hundreds of years old. In 1870 the Old House was occupied by William Glenny Andrews and two of his sisters Margaret and Mary, none of whom ever married. Uraghmore was the abode of Thomas of Ardara's mother Sarah, a daughter of the famous Dr William Drennan, supposedly one of the founders of the United Irishmen. Thomas himself would also have lived here before his marriage.

Thomas' uncle Isaac lived at the Big House in Comber Square which he bought in the 1840s from the insolvent William Stitt. At that time he had also demolished the house in which General Gillespie had been born, in order to extend his own house and garden. There are rumours that the workmen unearthed a hoard of gold treasure. Interestingly, Isaac's father had left him land at Carnesure and money to build a house there, provided he married.

But it was his nephew, Thomas' eldest brother James, who eventually built Carnesure House on the Killinchy Road in 1863, and this was his abode in 1870.

And what was the pedigree of Eliza, the blushing bride of 1870? Born in 1845 in Canada, she was two years younger than her new husband. Tragically, her father James died during a cholera outbreak in New York in 1849. There is a memorial inscription to him on the Andrews grave at Comber Non-Subscribing Church. Eliza's mother had been a Montgomery, a niece of Rev. Henry Montgomery, leader of the Non-Subscribing Presbyterian Church movement in the north of Ireland. She now decided to return to Ireland with her young family, which by this stage also included William James, born in 1847. He was the future Lord Pirrie, who in 1874 became a

Eliza Pirrie née Montgomery 1820–95

partner in the shipbuilding firm of Harland and Wolff in Belfast, and in 1895 chairman. He was also Lord Mayor of Belfast in 1896 and 1897. He died of pneumonia in Cuba in 1924 while on a business tour of South America. Interestingly, Lord Pirrie was a member of Comber Non-Subscribing Church, serving on its committee from 1879–93.

Eliza and her family lived at Conlig House, the home of her father-in-law, just outside Bangor. Around 1867 she had moved to a house called Aureen in Comber Square. Her sister-in-law Agnes Pirrie had lived here until her death in 1863, married to John Miller, the distiller. Eliza remained at Aureen until her children were happily married off. This would also have been the home of her daughter Eliza until 1870, although William James was in lodgings in Belfast where he already worked at the Harland and Wolff shipyard. He would have stayed at Aureen at weekends until his marriage in 1879 to Margaret Carlisle. Eliza senior eventually died in 1895.

4

Thomas Andrews Junior

Thomas Andrews Junior (or Tom as he was known) was born on 7 February 1873, the second son of Thomas of Ardara and Eliza Pirrie. Strangely, no record of his baptism has been found. We are told that he was a 'healthy, energetic, bonny child' who 'grew into a handsome, plucky and lovable boy'.

Ardara House, childhood home of Thomas Andrews Junior

Tom grew up at Ardara where he developed a very close relationship with his elder brother John Miller (born 17 July 1871). One of his occupations was that of beekeeping and he kept nine hives in the shelter of the hedge. He loved animals, and had a special passion for horses, becoming one of the most fearless riders in County Down. Even in these early days he was very fond of boats and enjoyed sailing on Strangford Lough, earning the nickname of the 'Admiral'.

Tom attended the family church – Comber Non-Subscribing Presbyterian, participating in its various activities such as the Sunday School. His life was grounded in the Christian faith, and his church would remain important to

Telescope of 'Admiral Tommie'

him. Throughout his life he would never touch alcoholic drink or smoke a cigarette.

Until the age of eleven Tom was educated privately by a tutor, but from 1884 to 1889 he attended the Royal Belfast Academical Institution (Inst). Here he was one of the most popular boys in his class, but he showed no special aptitude for study and was much fonder of games, especially cricket and hockey, at both of which he excelled. Comber, of course, has great cricketing traditions, being home to North Down Cricket Club.

Tom made his first appearance for North Down in 1887 as an enthusiastic fourteen year old. But because of his work commitments he never established himself in what was a very strong senior team. Rather, he became a prominent member of the 2nd XI, making the occasional appearance for the 1st XI. He was also a founder member of North Down Hockey Club in 1896.

Andrews family cricket XI which defeated the mighty North Down in 1895.
From back: Thomas Junior, Thomas James, John Junior, James, John Miller,
Oscar, Cecil, Ernest, Sydney, Arthur and Herbert

Census Returns 1901 and 1911

The Census return of 1901 for Town Parks, Comber, shows nine residents at Ardara – six members of the Andrews family and three servants.

Thomas, head of the family and a Flax Spinner, and his wife, **Eliza** are both noted as 'Unitarian' and able to read and write. Four of their unmarried children still live at home: **John Miller** (age 29 and a flax-spinner), **Eliza** (age 26), **James** (age 24 and a barrister in practice) and **William** (age 14 and at school). **Thomas**, as we shall see shortly, has already left home.

The three servants, interestingly, are all from what is now the Republic of Ireland – and educated. The cook, **Jane Irwin**, an Anglican, is 29 and from County Sligo. The house and parlourmaid, **Mary Peoples**, is 23 and is a Presbyterian from County Donegal; while the dairymaid, **Mabel Turbitt**, aged 20, is a Monaghan Presbyterian.

By 1911, only two of the children are still at home with their parents – **James** (now age 34 and a 'barrister in actual practice'), and **William** (now a flax-spinner master). **John Miller**, who married **Jessie Ormrod** in 1902, is now living just up the road at Maxwell Court, while **Eliza**, now **Mrs Lawrence Hind**, has settled with her husband in Nottinghamshire. At Ardara the family still retain educated servants – but these are three new staff. The cook now is the widowed **Jane Murray** and the parlourmaid is **Martha Jamison**, both County Down Presbyterians; while the laundress is **Katherine Gillespie**, a Roman Catholic from County Londonderry. There is no longer a dairymaid living at Ardara.

In the 1901 Census return for the Windsor Ward, Antrim, we find **Thomas Andrews Junior** lodging in Wellington Place, Belfast. Having left Ardara to pursue his career in the shipyard, he would have found this house very convenient and central. His landlady, a Unitarian dressmaker, is **Jane Scott**, a 50 year old spinster from County Down. Her sister, **Hannah Scott** shares the house and is a teacher. What brought these two sisters and their servant, a married Welsh Presbyterian called **Hannah Fallan**, to Belfast, we will never know – but we can imagine these three ladies took great care of their lodger. **Thomas**, now 28, is working as Assistant Shipyard Manager.

Ten years bring a change in **Thomas**' circumstances. By 1911, now a married shipbuilder, he lives with his young wife **Helen**, in their home – Dunallen in Windsor Avenue, at that time, No. 12, but nowadays No. 20. Their daughter, **Elizabeth**, just a baby, has been raised, like her mother, in the Church of Ireland faith, unlike **Thomas** who remains a Unitarian. **Bessie Abernethy** from County Tyrone has been hired as the baby's nursemaid – and there are four other female servants – all educated. The cook, **Helon Lee**, is a married Presbyterian from County Mayo, while the parlourmaid, **Mary Doyle** from Wexford, housemaid, **Margaret Jones** from Louth, and general domestic, **Lizzie Scott** from County Antrim, are all Church of Ireland.

It is sad to reflect that this was the last time the name 'Thomas Andrews' would appear on any census reports.

On leaving school in May 1889 at the age of sixteen, Tom joined Harland and Wolff as an apprentice. This necessitated a move to lodgings in Belfast during the working week, returning home at weekends.

In the 1901 Census, aged 28, by now with the rather important sounding title of Assistant Shipyard Manager, he is to be found living at 11 Wellington Place. From here he would have taken the tram to his work, or perhaps even walked on occasion. And at some stage he joined Rosemary Street church, although he also continued to worship at home in Comber whenever possible.

Tom showed great enthusiasm for his new job. As an apprentice he moved round all the different departments of the shipyard, gaining an excellent knowledge of all aspects of shipbuilding, and supplemented this practical experience with a course of night studies. But it was in the Drawing Office that he found his true *forte*, and Tom became involved in the design of many of the great ships of his day, starting in 1893 with the *Mystic*. By 1904 he was Assistant Chief Designer and the following year head of the Designing Department. In 1907 he was made a managing director of Harland and Wolff, of which his uncle was head.

In 1908 Tom married Helen Reilly Barbour in Lambeg Parish Church. Helen was from a well-known Dunmurry family, who like that of Tom had

Thomas Junior's wedding to Helen Barbour of Dunmurry – 24 June 1908

made their money in the linen industry. They went to live at a house called Dunallen, at Windsor Avenue in Belfast, and Tom is sometimes referred to as Thomas of Dunallen. There was one daughter, Elizabeth Law Barbour Andrews, born in 1910.

Harland and Wolff constructed many ships for the White Star Line, ships like *Oceanic, Celtic, Cedric, Baltic, Adriatic, Olympic* and *Britannic*, and these were among the largest vessels of their day, built to withstand the perils of trans-Atlantic crossings. *Titanic* was the mightiest of all. Construction started in 1909, with the launch on 31 May 1911. By early 1912 work was complete and *Titanic* left Belfast for Southampton and its first voyage to the New World. Tom was on board.

Unfortunately, *Titanic* did not make it to America. The iceberg saw to that. And Tom did not come back. But he will never be forgotten, especially in his home town of Comber. We will look at Comber's memorials later.

Wedding jacket of Thomas Andrews Junior
modelled by Michael Andrews

Launch of the *Oceanic* 1899, largest ship in the world in its day

5

Comber 1912

But first, what sort of town was the Comber of 1912? Let us pick up our tour guide and find out.

Welcome to Comber, or 'Comar' – the place where the waters meet. This may refer to the confluence of the Enler and Glen, which merge at the bottom of Park Way to form the Comber River. Equally possible is the meeting of the Comber River with Strangford Lough – the 'strang fjord of the Vikings'.

St Mary's Parish Church in Comber Square

WALKING TOUR MAP KEY

1. St Mary's Parish Church
2. Gillespie Monument
3. Bank
4. Engineering Works
5. Londonderry School
6. The Big House
7. Glebe House
8. Aureen
9. Site of Barry's Inn
10. 2nd Comber Church
11. Upper Distillery
12. The Cooperage
13. Potale Lane
14. Market House
15. St Mary's R.C. Church
16. Level Crossing
17. Milling's Yard
18. Paragon Pub
19. Distillery Houses
20. 1st Comber Church
21. Non-Subscribing Church
22. Andrews Mill
23. Mill School
24. Level Crossing
25. Ardara
25a. To Maxwell Court
26. Orange Hall
27. Inla
28. Masonic Hall
29. Railway Station
30. Railway Tavern
31. Thompson Hall
32. Corn Mill (disused)
33. Gasworks
34. Cricket Club
35. Flour Mill
36. Beetling Mill
37. Old Corn Mill
38. Grain Store
39. Castle
40. To Kennel Bridge
41. House of Industry
42. Barrack Row
43. The Old House
44. Gardens
45. Uraghamore
46. Masonic Hall
47. Methodist Church
48. Newtown Bridge
49. Lower Distillery Dam
50. Lower Distillery

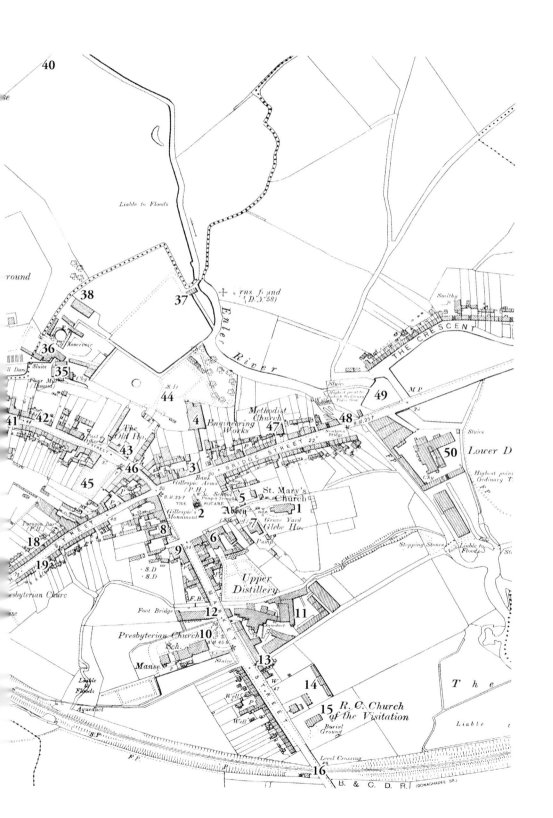

St Mary's Parish Church just off the Square is an appropriate starting point for any tour of Comber. It was on this site that a Cistercian monastery was built in 1199. During the Middle Ages this would have been a thriving community, but it was closed in 1543 by order of Henry VIII. Look for traces of the monastery in re-used stones in nearby walls and buildings. At least one of these had a mason's mark inscribed on it in the form of a cross. The Scots settlers established a church around 1610 in the ruins of the monastery, but the present St Mary's dates from 1840. The rector is Charles Campbell Manning, who replaced the late Canon George Smith last year (1911).

Points of interest:

Inscription on entrance pillar into grounds. The names of Thomas Andrews and James Lemont, churchwardens, are recorded, along with the date 1774. These men paid for the erection of the pillars.

The Andrews Mausoleum, built in 1867 by William Glenny Andrews over the family burial ground. We have already studied this.

The graveyard contains many early headstones, some from the 17th century. One interesting inscription relates to William Murdoch, the 'eminent distiller of Comber', who died in 1805.

Look out also for a red limestone slab at the front of the church in memory of Isaac Meredith of Kilbreght who died in 1723. Judge for yourself whether he really lived to the grand old age of 127 years.

Also at the front of the church is a plaque in commemoration of Edmund Bennett, an early minister. As you will observe, Mr Bennett was also chaplain to the Earl of Mount Alexander. The first earl was the grandson of Viscount Montgomery of the Ardes. He took his name from Mount Alexander Castle, a large manor house in Castle Lane, long since gone.

As you enter the church, look up to the top of the stairs and note two old stone tablets (once one piece) inscribed with initials, mottoes and the dates 1633 and 1637. What do they signify?

Note the font, which is very old and made of porphyry, a stone found in Mediterranean countries.

Many old monuments are worth studying. Of major importance is the memorial to Captain Chetwynd, Lieutenant Unite and Ensign Sparks, 3 officers of the York Fencibles killed at the Battle of Saintfield during the 1798 Rebellion. Incidentally, Rev. Robert Mortimer, the rector of Comber, was also killed at this battle.

A new North Transept is almost completed, and is to be dedicated in 1913 in memory of Canon George Smith, rector from 1868 to 1911.

Proceed across the Square to the Gillespie Monument, remembering that this area is an ancient graveyard belonging to the monastery. Sir Robert Rollo Gillespie (1766–1814) is Comber's famous general, whose statue stands on top of a 55-foot high Grecian column. His birthplace was demolished in the 1840s and rumour has it that the workmen discovered a hoard of gold. Gillespie fought against the French and their allies in the West Indies, India and Indonesia. His ride from Arcot to Vellore in 1806 was the subject of a poem by Sir Henry Newbolt (see Appendix 2). Gillespie was killed outside the fortress of Kalunga in Nepal in 1814. His reputed, but doubtful, last words (recorded on the Monument) were 'One shot more for the honour of Down'. He is buried at Meerut in India.

Unveiling of Gillespie Memorial 1845

Points of interest:

The monument was unveiled on 24th June 1845 (St John's Day) in front of an estimated 30,000 people. Gillespie was a freemason, and the monument has much Masonic symbolism, even down to the direction in which he faces.

The names of all Gillespie's major battles are inscribed on the sides of the column, from Tiburon in 1794 to Kalunga in 1814.

The date of Gillespie's death is given wrongly on the Monument as 24th October. It was actually 31st October.

Also recorded on the monument is another Sir Robert Rollo Gillespie, another general who fought in India. He was the grandson of the man on the statue.

There is another monument to Gillespie, inside St Paul's Cathedral, London, by the sculptor Sir Francis Chantrey.

The old wooden hut beside the Gillespie Monument is rather an eyesore. It is derisively called the Market House but is in reality a building to house the weighbridge for the Distillery where farmers bring their grain to be weighed.

Take some time to study the Square, which is largely Georgian in origin. Note the houses on the north side with sentry-box doorways. The Northern Bank, established in 1850, is housed in another rather impressive looking Georgian building. The bank manager is James Park Cinnamond. The front part of the bank is mid 18th century, but it was extended to the rear around 1840, probably by Dr Jonathan Allen. Beside it, on the site of an old tannery, are the traction engine works of James George Allen.

The old Londonderry School building occupies much of the east side of The Square. It was founded in 1813 by Lady Londonderry and the Erasmus Smith Foundation. Mr William H. Spence has been principal of the school since 1897.

The south side of the Square is dominated by the Big House built by the Stitt family and taken over by Isaac Andrews in the 1840s. It was Isaac's sons who founded the Belfast flour mills of Isaac Andrews & Sons. The Stitt family once had a small spinning mill at the rear of the building. Mrs Andrews, widow of Thomas James who died in 1908, lives in the Big House today. The glebe house or rectory, built 1738, sits between the Big House and St Mary's. A new rectory is being built at Laureldale.

On the west side is the home and business of the Milling family, one of the oldest traders in Comber, established in 1731. The house called Aureen was formerly the home of John Miller (1796–1883), owner of Comber Distilleries. Note the cobbled pavement. You will see John Miller's name picked out in white stone; also a dog chasing a hare, along with the figure of a man. Some surmise the dog to be the champion greyhound Master McGra, owned by Lord Lurgan. (His cousin James Brownlow was agent for Lord Londonderry). It may, however, simply be a hunting scene.

Let us now investigate Killinchy or Market Street, earlier known as Barry Street. Barry's Inn once sat at the corner next to Aureen. Early meetings of the Non-Subscribing Church were held in Barry's barn. At the first of these in 1837 Dr Montgomery preached for two hours. Proceed along the street until you see Second Comber Presbyterian Church on the right. The date 1839 was when the foundation stone was laid and John Rogers installed as the first minister. In 1838 around 70 families had broken away from First Comber because of disagreement about the new minister there. Behind is the Smyth Schoolhouse and Manse. A plaque inside the schoolhouse commemorates the financial gift from John Smyth of New Comber House towards the building of the manse (1860) and the schoolhouse (1861). James McCrea is principal of the School. The minister of the church is Rev. Thomas McConnell, who was installed in 1911.

Upper Distillery dam (now church car park) with
2nd Comber manse and schoolhouse behind

Opposite Second Comber is the Old or Upper Distillery, which has manufactured the famous Old Comber Whiskey since the 18th century. It has been owned by Samuel Bruce since 1871, when he bought it from John

Comber's Market House, Killinchy Street

Miller. Across the road is the Cooperage where they make the barrels. The distillery dam is just beyond Second Comber Church. Water flows from the Glen River into the dam along an aqueduct called the Troughs (pronounced trows).

Go down Potale (pronounced potyal) Lane beside the Distillery, towards the River Enler. Potale is the remains of the barley after the distilling process and is sold to farmers for cattle feed. Another name is Waterford Loney, as the lane leads down to a ford over the river at the spot where the Glen and Enler Rivers meet.

Return to Killinchy Street and turn left past the Market House, which now belongs to the Distillery. The Roman Catholic Church of the Visitation of the Blessed Virgin opened for worship in 1872. Prior to this, mass had been celebrated in the Market House and earlier still in Lower Crescent. A school was opened in 1904. Father James McAuley was appointed as parish priest of Newtownards and Comber earlier this year in succession to Father George Crolly. Turn at the railway level crossing where the Belfast and County Down Railway (BCDR) crosses the road on its way to Newtownards, and retrace your steps to the Square.

Proceed up High Street, the Coo Vennel or Cow Lane of the Scots settlers. Near the bottom of the street, on the right hand side, is Milling's Yard, and it was here in the upper room of an old outhouse that Second Comber first met in 1838. The Paragon Pub was opened by John W. Ritchie in 1900. In 1837 a total of 19 pubs is recorded in Comber. John McCance, the Presbyterian minister of the time, attributed to them 'almost all the wickedness and misery that surround us'. Mr Ritchie was also a merchant and grocer, as well as funeral undertaker. He had been appointed as Chairman of the Committee in charge of building the Thomas Andrews Junior Memorial Hall, but he has just died. Many of the houses in High Street, Braeside, Carnesure Terrace, Railway Street and Brownlow Street were built as mill houses by the Andrews family.

At the top of the hill is First Comber Presbyterian Church. The congregation was traditionally founded in 1645, but there was probably no church building here until around 1670. The date of 1645 coincides with the arrival of a Presbyterian minister called James Gordon in Comber, but Gordon was minister at St Mary's Parish Church! Until, that is, he was ejected and imprisoned. A crowd of women attacked his replacement, William Dowdall, in the church and pulled off his robes.

In 1764 there were 1,220 Presbyterians in Comber, compared with 315 members of the Established Church of Ireland and 165 Papists. Major building work took place in 1740 and 1887, and at this latter date the balcony and outside steps were removed. Government troops were quartered in the church after their defeat at the Battle of Saintfield in 1798. The outer wall of the First Comber National Schoolhouse records the date 1866 and the name of the Rev. Killen, minister 1843–79. Rev. Killen was minister at the time of the Great Revival of 1859 when many people at the church were reduced to tears on account of their sins and some had to be removed after fainting. The current minister is Rev. Dr Thomas Graham, who was installed in 1888. William Pollock replaced James Millen as headmaster of the school earlier this year.

The Non-Subscribing Presbyterian Church opened 1840

Just beyond First Comber is Windmill Hill, so called because there was once a windmill there. Make your way down the lane and through the gates of the Non-Subscribing Church. This was another breakaway group from First

Comber in 1837 and it is known as a Remonstrant congregation, because they remonstrated against compulsion to subscribe to the Westminster Confession of Faith. James Andrews donated the land on which the church was built. John Miller the distiller was another great benefactor and in 1871 had the church finished in Portland cement all at his own expense. The church was due to open in 1839, but in January of that year disaster struck on the night of the Big Wind. The top blew off the windmill on to the roof of the newly-built church causing severe damage. The church was unable to open for worship until 1840, making it the third church in Comber to open in that year. The first minister was William Hugh Doherty who emigrated to America in 1850. The graves of his two young sons can be found at St Mary's. The manse dates from 1859 and the schoolhouse from 1878. The unusual tree outside the church is a monkey-puzzle tree. In the graveyard which was consecrated in 1863, you will find the grave of John Miller. The minister is Rev. Thomas Dunkerley, installed in 1879.

View down Braeside towards the Andrews flax spinning mill *c.* 1900

Retrace your steps to High Street and proceed down Braeside to the flax-spinning mill of John Andrews & Sons. This was the brainchild of John Andrews (1792–1864), who was also agent for Lord Londonderry, who owned the town. It opened in June 1864, but John had died a few weeks before and it was left to his sons to carry on, especially Thomas (of Ardara) who had supervised the building work. Not all parts of the mill date from 1864; the earliest bit is the 4-storey Preparing and Spinning Rooms with a date stone of 1863. There are other date stones around the building e.g.

1907. The mill employs over 500 people. There is also a school attached to the Mill, and over a doorway is the inscription 'Comber Spinning Mill National Schools' and the date 1877. The principal of the Mill School is John Murray, appointed in 1890.

The main line of the Belfast and County Down Railway crosses the Ballygowan Road on a level crossing. Further along the Ballygowan Road are Ardara House, greatly extended in 1904 by Thomas Andrews (of Ardara), and Maxwell Court, the home of his son John Miller Andrews. Turn into Railway Street, so-called because the railway line runs along the right-hand side. The houses on the left-hand side were built by the Andrews family for their workers. Also on the left-hand side is Comber Orange Hall, the foundation stone of which was laid in 1875. The Hall opened in 1877. Just past it is a large house called Inla, home of Mr H.P. Andrews. Another short distance and you will see the Masonic Hall, opened 1870.

Comber Railway Station

Cross over the Glen Road to Comber Railway Station. The railway came to Comber in 1850, and Comber is an important junction with the main line from Belfast going via Ballygowan to Downpatrick and Newcastle while the branch line goes to Newtownards and Donaghadee. The express train to Belfast takes just 12 minutes! The platforms are 832 feet long, the longest on the entire BCDR system. Mr David John Johnston is stationmaster.

Go under the bridge and past the Railway Tavern, owned by Mr Todd, before proceeding into Mill Street. On your right is the Thompson Hall, provided in 1904 by John Thompson, a local entrepreneur, as a community and dance hall. Nearby is the Pound Bridge, so called because it was beside the Pound for stray animals. In Laureldale can be seen the ruins of the Upper Corn Mill, taken over by Thomas Andrews the miller in 1722.

Further along the street you will come to Comber Gasworks, which was previously a quarry belonging to John Andrews. The gasworks opened in 1847, and provides gas for many houses and other buildings in Comber, as well as street lighting. The manager is Joseph Hedley.

Laying out linen on the bleach green

Turn into Castle Lane and stroll down to the ground of North Down Cricket Club. This was originally a bleach green established in 1745 by John Andrews the Great, and in 1763 we are told that 2,000 pieces of linen were bleached here. We also read of it being robbed on occasion, even though the penalty was death by hanging. The cricket club was formed in 1857. They are 10 times senior cup winners and 5 times league champions. The pavilion was opened in 1909.

You will see many derelict and ruined buildings of the former industrial complex belonging to the Andrews family. This includes ruins of an impressive 5-storey flour mill dating from 1771, which closed in 1883, and also a beetling mill which was where they put a fine finish on linen cloth. On the banks of the Enler is the Old Mill from the 17th century, while a huge 6-storey grain store built in 1863 is now being used by a Dutchman named Stem for the manufacture of rice starch.

Further down Castle Lane was Mount Alexander Castle (a manor house rather than a castle), now gone. It was built as a wedding present by Hugh Montgomery, Viscount Ardes, for his son and his wife, Lady Jean Alexander, hence the name. Close by is the five-arch Kennel Bridge, which takes its name from the former kennels at the nearby castle.

Return along Castle Lane to its junction with Mill/Castle Street and turn left. Just across the street is a building containing Woods' drapers shop. This was once the House of Industry (an early workhouse), established in 1826 for 30 inmates. It also supported 70 outdoor families with meat and potatoes. Poor House Lane runs alongside the building. Barrack Row is the name for the line of houses on the left which includes the police station, which transferred to here from Bridge Street in 1861.

Make your way to the Old House of John Andrews (built 1745). Herbert Andrews now lives here. Behind are extensive walled gardens right down to the River Enler. Across the road is another Andrews house built by James in 1792 – Uraghmore, the place of the big yew trees, named after large trees in the garden believed to be several hundred years old. This is now the home of Annie Andrews, widow of John Andrews JP, who died in 1903.

Proceed past Comber's second Masonic Hall (opened 1906) back to the Square, and then walk down Bridge Street to the Methodist Church, built 1820. The porch was added in 1891. Further along you will cross the River Enler. Note the inscription on the bridge 'erected 1843 Edward Porter contractor'. A run-off from the river takes water into the Lower Distillery dam. The Distillery itself is on the other side of the Newtownards Road. Because it is surrounded by water (the Enler on one side, the run-off from the dam on the other) it is sometimes referred to as the Island Distillery.

Finally, take a stroll along the Crescent, sometimes called Hen Dung Row because of the number of hens kept by the inhabitants and the inevitable consequences. This was originally the route taken by the main road to Newtownards.

The Crescent or 'Hen Dung Row'

6

The People of Comber

Information on Comber and its inhabitants can be found in the *Belfast and Ulster Directories*. You will find copies of those for 1870 and 1912 as Appendices 3 and 4.

During the 1873–1912 lifetime of Thomas Andrews Junior, his home town of Comber developed rapidly as industry and economy brought improvements and new prosperity: in fact, a Traders' Association was formed during the period. At this time, Thomas' father served as Chairman of Comber Gas Light Company and the Belfast and County Down Railway.

A comparison of the street directories of 1870 and 1912 shows that life in Comber revolved mainly round the milling and whiskey industries, and the population increased as more people began to work, worship and send their children to school in the town. As a Plantation village, it is interesting to note that letters from Scotland arrived at Comber Post Office each morning at 8am – and replies were despatched by 5pm to be in time for the Scottish boats. Ties between Comber and Scotland were obviously close and no doubt many letters mentioned the shipbuilding industries of Belfast and the Clyde … The 1912 directory notes that the mail was carried on the County Down Railway line …

In 1870, five places of worship are recorded in the town – but by 1912, a Salvation Army Hall has appeared in Mill Street, with services at 3pm and 7pm. It is unusual that the 1912 Directory fails to mention St Mary's Roman Catholic Church in Killinchy Street – known, in 1870, as 'Downpatrick Street'. It is also worth pointing out that although Comber had several schools during this period, the only ones recorded are Erasmus Smith's School in the Square and an Infant School in Downpatrick Street …

The 1870 Directory separates out the 'Gentry, Clergy, Etc' from the other inhabitants of Comber, a segregation no longer made by 1912 – at least not in writing! The Andrews family dominate the list, with homes in the Square, Inla, Ardara, Uraghmore, Maxwell Court, The Old House and, of course, their various businesses throughout the town. Other members of the 1870

'Gentry' include George Allen of Unicarville (deceased by 1912), William Boyd of Ballywilliam Flax Mills (deceased by 1912), John Miller (Distiller, the Square, deceased by 1912), and Samuel Stone JP of Barnhill (still living in 1912) ... It is reasonable to surmise that Thomas would have known all these gentry well ...

It is also interesting to note the occupations prevalent amongst the traders of Comber – mostly revolving round farming and the cottage industries: in 1870, as well as the millers and distillers, we find surgeons, police constables and Inland Revenue officers, tanners, grocers, leather-cutters, saddlers, milliners, watch-makers, dress-makers, spirit-dealers (quite a few of these!), sewed muslin manufacturers, dyers, letter carriers, blacksmiths, drapers, tailors, carpenters, butchers, wheelwrights, cabinet-makers, bank managers, shoe-makers and grain merchants.

By 1912, the town has acquired book-keepers, glass and china merchants, coal merchants, civil engineers, stone-masons, accountants, gas-fitters, printers and stationers, timber and iron yard weighmasters, a steam-thresher proprietor, clothes dealers, druggists, cycle agents, funeral undertakers, a 'noted house for boots and shoes, hosiery, corsets, ladies' and children's underclothing etc', insurance agents, and fancy goods dealers: not to mention even more spirit-dealers! We can see how, during this period – a time when many of Comber's sons worked in the shipyard and commuted to Belfast on the BCDR, the town has become more sophisticated, with luxury goods starting to appear in the shops.

Thomas Andrews Junior had reason to be proud of his town: Comber, during his life, had become a self-sufficient, industrious and upwardly-mobile mill-town whose inhabitants knew how to both work and play.

Flax Spinning Mill

When Thomas Andrews Junior was born in 1873, the Flax Spinning Mill of John Andrews and Co. had been operating for almost nine years. It was in June 1864 that the mill had opened on the Ballygowan Road, the brainchild of Thomas' grandfather John, but he never lived to see his dream factory working. Sadly he had passed away a few weeks before the machinery sprang into life. It was therefore left to his sons James, John and Thomas to carry on the business, especially Thomas. This was Thomas of Ardara, father of Thomas Junior, the shipbuilder. The elder Thomas eventually became chairman in 1909 when the firm was made into a limited company.

This picture shows the original mill of 1864, taken from an *Illuminated Address* of that year, presented to the widow of John, the founder, by the

Flax Spinning Mill from an *Illuminated Address*. Note the train in right foreground

tenants of Lord Londonderry's estate, for which he had been agent. A major incentive for building was the American Civil War, because of which cotton was no longer available. Linen was an excellent alternative. Over the years there would be additions to the complex. The first new work was in the period 1875–7 with the erection of a block at the north end containing the boiler house. The schoolhouse was also added as an upper floor to an existing building at this time. Then in 1899 came a new engine house, and it is probable that the present chimney dates from this time. A Preparing Mill (for preparing the flax for spinning) followed in 1901, originally a single storey building but later a second floor was added. In 1907 there was a major extension to the main four-storey mill building. Thomas Andrews and his son John Miller, who was a junior partner, were also prepared to invest heavily in new plant and machinery to improve the quality and range of yarns. The Mill was obviously prospering, producing linen yarn rather than any finished articles. It had its own railway siding off the Belfast and County Down Railway which enabled the transport of coal, flax and yarn to and from the mill.

Flax was originally mostly grown locally, including on the Andrews' lands around Comber. The picture shows it stooked at Maxwell Court on the Ballygowan Road. However, as time went by consignments came from all over Ireland and even from as far away as Russia and Belgium. After 1910 it

Flax stooked in the fields near Maxwell Court, Comber

became scarce and extremely expensive. The directors had to work hard to keep the orders coming in and the workers in employment.

Flax was pulled by hand and then put into little ponds called lint holes for a process known as retting. This rotted and softened the stems of the plant and broke down the pectin, a substance which held together the flax fibre, woody core and outer cover. The process produced a noxious smell as the flax fermented. The flax was then drained in stooks on the banks of the lint hole and laid out to dry in the open air.

When the flax fibre was brought to the Mill, it would be combed by the roughers to straighten it out in preparation for spinning. The next stage was hackling, a further combing process in which the fibres were untangled, removing any remaining useless matter. The yarn at this stage looked something like human hair and was now ready for spinning. The wet spinning process involved a six hour soaking of the linen yarn in cold water to prevent it from snapping. It was the job of the doffers to ensure that the spinning frames were stopped at the appropriate time. They would then remove the full bobbins, throw them into boxes, and put empty bobbins on to the spindles. The full bobbins were then taken to the reeling room where the yarn was wound on to large revolving frames. It was then dried and made up into bundles for sale.

Some of the workers in Comber Flax Spinning Mill 1873 (fortnight ending 3 May)

Machine Room – John Blair, Samuel Smyth, James Hutton, James Murray, James Savage.

Preparing Room – Samuel McKeown, William Calwell, Agnes McMillan, Margaret Coey.

Spinning Room – Samuel Officer (presumably the man in charge – he was paid for 12 days at 6/8d per day, giving a gross pay of £4. Out of this was deducted 5/- for rent and 5/- for other items, giving a fortnightly take home pay of £3 10s). Other workers included Susanna Brown, Jane Cairns and Mary Dickson.

Doffers – Catherine Rankin, Jane Maxwell, Margaret Brown and Agnes Patton. (They were paid for 12 days at 10d a day plus 1s bonus, thus earning 11 shillings for the fortnight).

Reeling Room – Bella Bohil, Sarah Caughey, Agnes Robinson, Ellen Hutton.

Roughers – William Thompson, Robert Jellie, William O'Prey, John Cooper. Workers paid off during this fortnight were John McMillan, Hugh Jones, Thomas O'Prey and Matthew Brown.

Sorters – James Middleton, James Murphy, William Wilson, Samuel Carmichael.

Workers in the Reeling Room of Comber Mill

Some workers in the Spinning Room
(fortnight ending 12 November 1910)

> James Chambers (who appears to be the man in charge), Annie McDowell, Jane Anderson, Jane Mullan, Mary McKeag, Annie Lemon, Jane Cairns, Rachel Bennett.

Comber Distilleries

There were two distilleries in Comber producing the famous Old Comber Whiskey – the Upper Distillery in Killinchy (or Market) Street opposite Second Comber Presbyterian Church, and the Lower Distillery on the Newtownards Road, just beside where the library is today. Around 1860 both had come into the ownership of John Miller, who had been a partner in the Upper Distillery since 1826. Miller had retired in 1871 and sold the

Some artistic licence has been used in this poster advertising Old Comber whiskey

business to Samuel Bruce, an Englishman from Gloucestershire. Mr Bruce had also been the largest purchaser of the whiskey, which was sold at what was described in the *Down Recorder* as 'the largest auction of whiskey that has ever taken place in Belfast'. A Mr J. McCance Blizard was installed as a junior partner to look after the running of the business locally. He died in 1904.

During the period when Thomas Andrews Junior lived in Comber, Samuel Bruce owned the distilleries. 150,000 gallons of Old Comber whiskey were claimed to be produced from each distillery in 1887, enough to bring on many a hangover! The Prince of Wales (later King Edward VII) was among those who took a fancy to the stuff. Horses and carts were constantly making the trip to and from the railway station, loaded down with casks and jars for distribution far and wide. The firm was never particularly large, with around 60 employees and five Excise officers. It was their duty to ensure that the Government got their proper share of the revenue. In 1887 the chief Excise officer was Mr Thomas Galway.

The Upper Distillery was the larger of the two. Opposite was the cooperage where they made the barrels. A wages book of 1908 shows that coopers were

The still house at Comber Upper Distillery

top of the pay league at 5/7d a day. Stillmen and carpenters received a little
less. Worst paid were the women in the bottling plant on 2/- a day. By 1905
50% of sales were in bottles. Lots of water was required. This was diverted
from the Glen River along an aqueduct known as The Troughs (pronounced
trows) into a dam which is now the site of Second Comber Car Park. A petrol
filling station today occupies the site of a similar dam for the Lower Distillery.
It was fed by a run-off from the River Enler. Flooding in Bridge Street was
believed to be caused by high water levels as a result of a weir on the river.

Upper Distillery Yard, Potale Lane

Workers at the Lower Distillery *c.* 1915

Old Comber Whiskey was the product of a complex process. Grain was held in huge bins before grinding, after which the meal was conveyed to storage bins directly over the mash-tun in readiness for brewing. After this operation the liquor or wort was pumped to a tank in the refrigerating room from which it was piped to the tun room to ferment.

Only then did the actual distilling take place in the still-house where the fermented liquor was subjected to great heat, allowing condensation to take place. The vapour now commenced its quarter-mile journey through the 'worm' inside the worm-tub into which thousands of gallons of cold water per hour were poured. This ran out the other end at a very high temperature. The first sight of the liquid was through the glass sides of the spirit safe on its way to the low-wines still and the spirit receiver. From here it reached the spirit store vat at 50 degrees over proof, being reduced here to 25 degrees over proof, the usual bonding strength. The final stage involved filling the casks from the vat. These were rolled to the warehouse for maturing, sometimes up to 25 years.

Education

In 1912 there were five schools in Comber, four of which were connected with the churches of the town. The exception was the Mill School, and below we have a snapshot of the register for Comber Spinning Mill National School in 1910 showing pupils who joined between May and August in that year.

Extract from register of Spinning Mill School 1910

The Mill School opened in 1877. John Murray had been principal since 1890. In 1901 a total of 79 boys and 81 girls attended for examination. It was reported that 'the proficiency generally is very pleasing and marks a distinct advance on the work of last year'. And reports generally were very good – up until 1907 that is, when a new inspector arrived, the infamous W. MacMillan. He found that, although discipline was very good and the place well kept, 'not sufficient progress is made in Arithmetic, Geography and Grammar, the answering in these subjects being unsatisfactory. Pupils should be trained to answer in sentences. The Course in Kindergarten is exceedingly limited. The Monitor knew nothing of the history in her special course, her Grammar was also poor and she knew nothing of the British Possessions on the map'. Poor girl! By 1908 a new classroom had been built, although it was not yet furnished. Criticisms continued – 'A large class of Junior Infants should not be left to themselves as was the case at 11.30–12.00'. Imagine the chaos!

By 1910 all was well again, although there was still room for improvement:

> The school is well conducted, the pupils are obedient and attentive, and on the whole a very creditable proficiency has been reached. More care should be given to the tone in which the pupils answer questions; to the method of holding the sewing materials, and to the manner in which the action songs are rendered. The schoolrooms are bright and comfortable, and the playground is spacious and suitable.

Some of the teachers at the Mill School were Annie Moore, Lizzie J. Davis, Ann Caughey, Thomas Joseph Dailey, Ella Nora McKeag, Louisa Donnan, Caroline L. Murray, Gertrude E.M. Edgar, Minnie E. Martin and Ellen Jane Hoffman.

Here are a few observations noted by the inspector at the Londonderry National School at St Mary's in the Square, where the principal was William H. Spence, who had been appointed in 1897. Other teachers included Miss A. Bell, Miss Everina D. Drennan, Miss Lizzie Cunliffe and Miss Sarah O. Browne:

The Londonderry National School in Comber Square, dating from 1813

1904   The schoolroom is not sufficiently heated today.

1908   Train pupils to work silently when in desks and at arithmetic etc. There is often too much noise.

1910   The organisation and division of labour should be amended. At present, Principal is responsible for 18 pupils on rolls – and assistant for 81.

1911   The plants should be set out to get washed in the rain.

1912   Monitor's knowledge of history is very limited – her instruction should have been going on when I arrived.

William Pollock had just been appointed headmaster of First Comber National School in 1912, in succession to James Millen. Mr Millen in turn replaced James Chambers, principal from 1886 until 1908. First Comber was a big school with 208 pupils on the rolls in 1903. The inspector wrote that the members of the Teaching Staff were well qualified for their positions and most conscientious in the discharge of their duties, with the result that the pupils attending the school received an intelligent and effective training. His only criticism was 'I should like to see more attention given to mental and practical arithmetic.' However, by 1904 there was an unbelievable decline:

The children make too much noise when marching during a change. The pupils should not be permitted to draw with short pencils or to make too much use of rubbers. The children should not be permitted to spit on their slates and use their cuffs to clean them. The teacher should be provided with a piece of wet sponge with which to damp the slates, when the children wish to clean them. The teaching notes of the teachers should be prepared daily and suitably graduated; otherwise notes are of little value.

Assistant teachers included Miss Annie McCappin, Miss Barbara Proctor (whose father was manager of the Distillery), Miss Emily McKee and Miss Evelyn Maud Dunlop.

Second Comber was also known as Smyth's National School, after John Smyth of New Comber House who donated a sizable sum of money towards the erection of the schoolhouse in 1861. James McCrea had been principal since 1907. Previous headmasters included a Mr J.D. Harper, who was there in 1873, Mr Boyce, Mr J.B. Macrory (1887–94), Mr A.S. Harvey (1894–8) and Mr D.S. Hunter (1898–1906). Other teachers were Ella McKeag, John Gamble, Mary Thompson, Margaret Murdoch, Miss Kenning and Miss Crabbe.

Pupils of Smyth's School at Second Comber c. 1912

There were only two rooms in the school, which were fully occupied by nine classes. Mr McCrea taught Science, and it was reported that 'Satisfactory progress is being made in this branch, at the same time the full value is not obtained from the instruction unless practical work is done by the pupils'. In 1909 the teaching of needlework came in for scathing criticism:

> The garments, which are good, have occupied too much time. Forms (seats) should be arranged in parallel positions so that the whole class may see the teacher's demonstrations from a favourable position. Thorough training should be imparted to Juniors in drill form, in such exercises as holding materials for sewing, knitting, tacking, folding work etc. Cutting out, ironing etc should be introduced without delay.

Who would have been a teacher in those days when the inspector's function seems to have been to find fault?

St Mary's National (Roman Catholic) School was the newest in Comber, opening in Killinchy Street on 10 October 1904. Miss Susan Meehan was appointed principal teacher. In 1911 the Manager of the school (the priest) was requested to censure Miss Mary Wade, late principal who was now an assistant in Knockmahon National School, 'for her want of care in keeping the roll and report books'.

OPPOSITE PAGE:
The Frances Street offices of the
Newtownards Chronicle c. 1960s

THE NEWTOWNARDS
Chronicle
& CO. DOWN OBSERVER

What topics were discussed round the Andrews family table, or at the Cricket Club, or at Thomas' church? What issues would have engaged his mind? We have drawn up a diary of events in Comber during the period 1873–1912, setting them in the context of what was happening in the wider world.

Much of this information has been gleaned from the pages of the *Newtownards Chronicle*, the local newspaper covering a wide geographical span centred on the town of Newtownards and including the Ards Peninsula, Comber and areas of mid-Down as far away as Killyleagh and Ballynahinch. We are grateful to the editor of the *Chronicle* for permission to use this information.

The *Newtownards Chronicle* began publication in July 1873. There was a forerunner, the *Newtownards Independent*, established in July 1871 by a consortium of local businessmen, but it came to an end in January 1873 when the manager William Henry slipped on an orange peel and injured his leg. It was Mr Henry who owned the *Chronicle*, continuing as sole proprietor until his death in 1890, when he was succeeded by his sons J.S. and R.S. Henry. The newspaper remained in the hands of the Henry family until 1947 when it was purchased by the Alexanders of Bangor.

The *Newtownards Chronicle* offices have been in Frances Street since the paper was founded. Until recent years the premises housed printing works and a compositing room, along with the office and advertising staff, and editorial and photographic departments. However, advancements in technology saw all works departments transfer to Balloo Industrial Estate in the late 1990s.

7

A Diary of Comber Events
1873–1912

1873

World Events

- Death of the explorer and missionary David Livingstone.
- The North West Mounted Police Force is formed in Canada.
- Ashanti War breaks out in Africa.
- The cities of Buda and Pest unite to form the capital of Hungary.
- German occupation of France ends following the Franco-Prussian War.
- Leo Tolstoy writes *Anna Karenina*.
- Greenwich Royal Naval College opens.

Thomas Andrews Junior was born at the family home of Ardara, Comber on 7th February, the second child of Thomas Andrews of Ardara and Eliza Pirrie, who had been married on 15th September 1870 in Comber Non-Subscribing Presbyterian Church. His elder brother was John Miller Andrews, born on 17th July 1871. Strangely, we do not have a record of Thomas' baptism.

What a joyful occasion Thomas' birth must have been. But there was also much cause for sorrow in Comber. A fatal accident occurred on the Belfast and County Down Railway (BCDR) in May:

> A young man, McConnell, who resides near that town [Comber], but is engaged in business in Belfast, had been in Comber playing at a cricket match. In the evening the driver of the goods train from Belfast saw a dark object on the line and whistled, but before the train could be stopped the man was run down.

Rev. Stuart James Niblock, minister
of Second Comber 1873–77

A new minister was installed in Second Comber Presbyterian Church on 17th June. This was Stuart James Niblock, formerly of Riverside congregation in Newry. The installation was at 12 noon, which seems an unusual time to hold it; this was after all a Tuesday, when ordinary people would normally have been working. But then, this was another world from that to which we have grown accustomed and they did things differently. Dr Killen, minister of First Comber, congratulated the congregation 'on their choice of such a gifted and excellent minister.'

Rev. Niblock was not without his problems. For instance, Second Comber had written to Presbytery 'alleging that the congregation had never chosen Mr John Cairns and that he was not entitled to act as an elder in 2nd Comber'. There was also the matter of church music. A 'Lover of Good Music' wrote about 'the wretched state of the choir' and that 'the adoption of instrumental music would be a vast improvement to the present display of vocal powers'.

> I am afraid that the Music Question has been greatly neglected. Not many months since, hearings were had of a great many candidates for the precentorship of the above church, but to save the annual bounty of a small sum, a choir was organised, and how the music is conducted at present is too well known. I am credibly informed that Mr J.D. Harper, the present teacher of the National School in connection with Second Comber, conducts the psalmody in one of the leading churches in Belfast. Why not retain his services in the church to which his school is connected?

He also had a gripe about 'the miserable appearance of the pews of Second Comber. Now when the painters are engaged in the church, it would be a good opportunity either for the painting or staining of them …'

But no complaints about Sunday School numbers. At the end of the year it was reported that numbers on the roll had increased for 40 to 170.

The search for coal was well under way, as reported on 20th September:

> The search for coal which we announced lately as having been commenced near Comber has been continued and the depth now reached is upward of 60 feet. From the geological formation of the ground in which the operation has been made there is no expectation of the appearance of the coal bed, if any, for a considerable depth below that reached …

In fact, coal was never found.

Also in September, a farmer named Francis Boal from Ballyaltikilligan was in trouble with the law, and was summoned by Constable Robert Parker for 'unlawfully keeping a cow affected with the lung disease and neglecting to give notice to the constable in charge of Comber station'. He was fined 20 shillings for his misdemeanour.

A correspondent to the *Newtownards Chronicle* drew attention to the state of Comber Square:

> Perhaps some of your Comber correspondents could enlighten the public as to whose duty it is to keep the Square in such a condition that pedestrians may with safety pass over it. Formerly this was a handsome and pleasant place for the recreation of children, but since the miserable market shed was erected it has year by year been passing into a doubtful quagmire state.

An inquiry was held 'at the Crescent, Comber, into the death of a man named James Montgomery, who was found dead in a drain opposite his own house on the Newtownards Road, on Wednesday morning, at half past eight. Deceased was well-known, and generally respected, and had been in the employment of the County Down Railway Company for about twenty-four years'. A verdict was returned of accidental death, and it was pointed out that this was a dangerous spot where it was a wonder that more accidents did not occur.

1874

World Events

- Isaac Butt, MP for Limerick, proposes Home Rule for Ireland.
- Benjamin Disraeli defeats Gladstone in the General Election.
- Britain annexes Fiji.
- The rules of lawn tennis are drawn up.
- James Boot opens a chemist shop in Nottingham.
- Society for the Prevention of Cruelty to Children is founded in New York.
- Thomas Hardy book *Far From the Madding Crowd* is published.

Comber Old Standard LOL 567 held their annual soirée and ball on 30th January in Mr Henry Murdoch's barn:

> After a good tea being served round, dancing was commenced and kept up until an advanced hour on Saturday morning, when all separated, seeming highly pleased with their night's entertainment.

Thomas Andrews got a baby sister on 21st June with the birth of Eliza Montgomery Andrews. She would be known as Nina.

If only statues could speak! Sir Robert Rollo Gillespie got a few matters off his chest in a letter to the *Newtownards Chronicle*:

> I am sure, like all my old friends, you will be pleased to hear that I have got a new suit of beautiful drab, with white strips up and down and across, and don't I look A1? But when I look down from my elevated position, and sees that most detestable shade [shed], I am grieved, and wonder how any party ever could think of putting it there to disgrace me, and insult the noble and generous parties who put me here, and as everyone understands, no General requires a sentry-box. But if I could get down (as I cannot now; for the painters have taken away the ladders) I would get powder and send the whole edifice in true balloon style to the Glass Moss, where there is plenty of room, and few to see it but the goats, and it might be useful to the bearding in the winter time ...

Sir Robert Rollo Gillespie
1766–1814

'Market House' *c.* 1900. Note the iron railings round the Monument

The shed referred to once huddled in the shadow of Gillespie, an eyesore in the eyes of most people and derisively nicknamed the 'Market House'. In 1874 it belonged to the Distillery, and farmers would have their barley weighed here on a Thursday. It was eventually demolished prior to laying out the Memorial Gardens in the Square in 1952.

1875

World Events

- Charles Stuart Parnell makes his maiden speech in the House of Commons.
- Britain takes control of the Suez Canal.
- The use of children as chimney sweeps is outlawed in Britain.
- Captain Matthew Webb swims the English Channel.
- Chivers opens a jam-making factory in Cambridgeshire.
- Bizet's opera *Carmen* is first performed.
- Mark Twain writes *The Adventures of Tom Sawyer*.

A site was procured in Railway Street on which to build an Orange Hall. In May 'the farmers in the neighbourhood inaugurated their share of the work by carting upwards of fifty tons of stone from the quarries of Messrs Ritchie & Jackson'. The foundation stone was laid on Saturday 18th September:

> The chief stone of this Orange Hall, which is now in course of erection, was laid at three o'clock on Saturday last, in the presence of a large assemblage of the brethren and other Protestant friends. The building promises to be a very fine one, and will be two storeys in height, with a gable front. The site, which is adjacent to the railway station, was generously granted by the Marquis of Londonderry, through his esteemed agent, Mr James Brownlow, JP ... The stone was to have been laid by Mr Brownlow, but, owing to his unavoidable absence in England, the duty was deputed to his son, Mr Claude Brownlow. Numbers of the brethren marched, with flags and music, from Newtownards, Ballygowan, Ballymacarrett, Belfast, and the surrounding districts to the hall, so that, during the proceedings, there must have been several thousands present ... A substantial platform was erected, wherefrom the speakers addressed the meeting, and this was appropriately bedecked with flags and banners ...

The chairman at the proceedings was the Rev. George Smith, rector of St Mary's Parish Church, whose portrait is still to be seen on the banner of Comber True Blues LOL 1035. Speakers included the Rev. Mr Woods of Ballygowan and Mr Charles Ward of Belfast. Mr Arthur De Wind, the architect of the hall, also took part in the ceremony.

Head-Constable Parker was transferred on promotion to Newry, but in July, shortly before his departure, he performed one last heroic deed:

> On Wednesday evening, a child aged about 2½ years, son of a labourer named Isaac Reid, was playing at Castle Lane, Comber, when a pet pig, kept in the locality, ran at it, knocked it down, worried it about the head and arms, and undoubtedly would have killed it on the spot, were it not for the timely intervention of Head-Constable Parker and Sub-Constable McNamee, who were passing, and ran to the child's assistance. They succeeded in rescuing it after some difficulty. Dr Frame was called upon immediately, and found the child in a very precarious state, but it is hoped the injuries will not prove fatal.

Not so fortunate was James Kyle of Ringcreevy, who lost his life in a tragic accident in September:

> The deceased, who was an industrious, enterprising man, assisted by his son, had some time ago erected a scutch-mill … At about three o'clock on Thursday evening, he was seen going into the engine-room, and shortly after a cry of "murder" was heard by a little boy in the boiler room. The boy looked through the window, and saw the deceased revolving on the shaft. He immediately raised the alarm, and the men in the mill came rushing to the place, when a fearful sight presented itself.

The poor man's clothes had been torn off and wrapped round his right arm, fastening him firmly to the shaft, which was going at forty revolutions to the minute. And at each revolution his legs were striking against other parts of the machinery. Dr Frame was sent for, but to no avail. The unfortunate Mr Kyle died two hours later.

1876

World Events

- An Irish Home Rule Bill is defeated in the House of Commons.
- The Plimsoll Line is introduced on British ships.
- Alexander Graham Bell invents the telephone.
- Thomas Edison invents the phonograph [or gramophone].
- Queen Victoria is proclaimed Empress of India.
- The grey squirrel is introduced into Britain from America.
- US National Baseball League is formed.

In January Second Comber appointed their new committee for the coming year. But money was being illegally collected in the name of the congregation, and this had to be halted:

> A resolution bearing on the recent raids on the congregation by a few unauthorised persons going about in the name of the congregation collecting subscriptions was discussed by several members and was brought to a close by the chairman pointing out that such proceedings were unconstitutional and indicated that parties should have the sanction and approval of the session and committee before they take the liberty of acting in the name of the congregation.

We wonder what the record is for the number of lambs born to a sheep. In April one Comber sheep gave birth to four: 'The birth of 4 lambs to a sheep belonging to Andrew Smith, flesher, of Comber is recorded. All are healthy and likely to do well'.

The Andrews family flour-milling business was in difficulties, showing a loss of some £2,000 a year since 1868. A cousin of Thomas Andrews of Ardara, Isaac's son John, was persuaded to return from Liverpool to steady the sinking ship. By 1877 he had turned the deficit into a profit. During all this time it seems that the flax spinning mill continued to prosper under the capable hands of Thomas of Ardara and his brothers James and John.

The Mill excursion took place in August:

> On Saturday the workers in the extensive mill belonging to Thomas Andrews Esq, Comber, to the number of 500, held their annual excursion, the place selected being Newcastle. On their arrival they proceeded to Lady Annesley's demesne, where they spent a most enjoyable and happy day. Dancing to the music of the fine band of the Royal North Down Rifles was indulged in, and sports of different kinds diversified the day's proceedings … This affords us one more illustration of the good feeling existing between employer and employed in this district – a feeling as rare nowadays as it is commendable.

1877

World Events

- Britain annexes the Boer Republic of Transvaal in South Africa.
- Australia beat England at Melbourne in the first cricket test match (the Ashes).
- The first Lawn Tennis championships are held at Wimbledon.
- The University Boat Race between Oxford and Cambridge ends in a dead-heat.
- The moons and so-called canals of Mars are discovered.

Thomas Andrews' younger brother James was born on 3rd January. James would grow up to have an outstanding career in the legal profession, rising to become Lord Chief Justice of Northern Ireland.

James Milling of the Square, however, was concerned not so much with births as with deaths:

> He has added to his Undertaking Department a new hearse of the most modern construction, and is now prepared to execute all orders entrusted to him in first-class style. Coffins, oak and black, shoulder scarfs, hat bands, and every other article in connection with the above supplied.

Meanwhile, staff were sought for the Mill School:

> Teacher wanted. – A well qualified female teacher for a school about to be opened under the National Board, in connection with the Comber Spinning Mill. Apply immediately to John Andrews & Co, Comber.

The school opened in March with Kate White as the first principal. But by July she had been relegated to the position of assistant, with William Groves as principal.

Comber got a new stationmaster when John Kelly succeeded John Gaynor who had been appointed to Newtownards. Soon after this, on 6th June, tragedy struck on the railway:

> On Wednesday morning a melancholy and fatal accident took place on the County Down Railway, on the Killinchy side of this town,

Killinchy Street railway level crossing

where there is a level railway crossing on the main road leading from Comber to Killinchy. The nine o'clock train from Newtownards to Belfast was a few minutes late in leaving this station; but all went well to nearing the crossing referred to, when the driver observed the gates shut, and gave the usual danger whistle. Mrs Agnes Withers, the woman who has charge of the crossing, ran out, but got confused, and before the second gate was opened the engine was upon her, and struck her on the side. Death was almost instantaneous. Both gates have been partially smashed. The deceased was about fifty years of age.

At an inquest held shortly afterwards it was recommended that women should not be employed to look after the gates at level crossings. How acceptable would this verdict be in our modern society with its emphasis on equality legislation in the workplace?

The Orange Hall was officially opened on Sunday 1st July by Rev. J.D. Crawford of Hillhall. In September the lodges moved in to their new home:

> At half past seven o'clock the brethren composing lodges 244, 567, 1035 assembled in Brother Ward's in Mill Street, and from thence, accompanied by the flags, fifes, and drums of their respective lodges, they proceeded to Bridge Street, where they met the brethren of lodge 1037. Having re-formed there, they proceeded to the Square and marched round the monument erected to General Gillespie, and thence to Mill Street, and to the hall, where they spent the remainder of the evening in transferring the "properties" of the different lodges from their old to their new quarters. It should be stated that an old and respected member of the Orange institution – Mr David McMaster – was chaired and carried in triumph by a number of the brethren from Mill Street to the door of the Orange Hall.

Meanwhile the Twelfth had been held at Barnhill on the Belfast Road in a field belonging to Mr Samuel Stone.

> Thursday was celebrated with the usual honours at Comber and Newtownards. From an early hour in the morning the fifes and drums were heard through the streets, and the usual excitement prevailed.

But it was generally felt that the field was not well situated, not having the usual commanding position chosen for such occasions. It was divided in two by the railway line, and the grass had not even been cut in the part where the platform was erected. And there were a few hitches:

On nearing Comber the Newtownards districts were met by the Comber lodges, and here another hitch occurred as some of the lodges should have gone in the Belfast and others in the Newtownards direction to meet the contingents from the respective places, but in this they failed as they preferred the latter route.

Comber Orange Hall, officially opened 1877 and demolished 2009

In those days the Newtownards and Belfast lodges marched all the way to Comber. Speakers included Rev. George Smith of Comber, James Jeffrey of Newtownards and Rev. Joseph Dickson of Mariner's Church, Belfast.

Rev. Niblock of Second Comber was off to pastures new:

> … Mr Niblock having accepted the pastorate of Newark Church, Port Glasgow, and demitted the charge of the second congregation of Comber, the Presbytery regret losing his brotherly fellowship and valuable counsels and services, desire him an abundant measure of success, by Divine grace, in his new field of labour, and furnish him with credentials declaratory of his personal character and official position.

Rev. David A. Taylor was ordained as his replacement on 4th December. He was the son of a Belfast merchant and had been licensed by the Belfast Presbytery in 1876.

Also in December, the Rev. John Orr of the Non-Subscribing Church was honoured by his congregation at a special soiree, chaired by John Miller, one of its founding fathers. An address was presented to Rev. Orr, and he was given a pay rise, the first substantial increase since his arrival in 1850.

The year ended with a shooting accident:

> An investigation was held by the magistrates regarding the death of Alexander Hill, The Crescent, Comber, who died on the 19th December from the effects of a pistol shot from a revolver … Mrs Hill and John Buchanan were examined, and stated that a young man named George McCaw, a relative of the deceased, called in his house, and showed him a small revolver which the deceased took in next door to show to Mr Adair, and while the latter was using it, not thinking it was loaded, the contents of one of the barrels lodged in Hill's abdomen. The dying deposition of the deceased, taken before Mr Miller, JP, was read, in which Hill acquitted Adair of all evil intents against him, and he was satisfied it was an accident.

What a way to go!

1878

World Events

- The Treaty of San Stefano secures peace in the Balkans.
- Britain occupies Cyprus.
- 268 miners are killed in a gas explosion at Abercarn in Wales.
- Over 600 are drowned when a pleasure steamer sinks in the Thames.
- Gilbert and Sullivan produce *HMS Pinafore*.
- The Salvation Army is founded with William Booth as general.
- The earliest electric street lighting appears in London.
- A new Eddystone Lighthouse is built.

Comber's version of the Olympic Games was held on Easter Monday:

> Splendid weather favoured the Comber athletic sports on Monday last, when the attendance was by far the best ever seen at this popular meeting. The sports were of an excellent description, the entries numerous for every race, and in more than one instance the finish was very closely contested. The first event on the programme was a donkey

race. Three came to the post, M. Boal's "Pasha", B. Long's "Ardmillan Maid", and C. Glover's "Blackball". Betting on the race was 5 to 4 on "Pasha", who got best away and won easily, "Ardmillan Maid" being second. The people then adjourned to a field kindly granted by T. Andrews Esq., for the remainder of the sports … Great amusement was caused by the boys in the sack, barrow, and three-leg races, which were kept up till late in the evening. Several unsuccessful attempts were made to gain the coveted prize of a purse of money on the top of a greased pole, which was placed on the bank of a river, and at last was only obtained by a good ducking in the adjoining river by S. Quinn. The sports were brought to a close by a grand display of fireworks from the railway bridge.

Comber was expanding:

Mr Robert Todd, Mill Street, Comber, has during the past few years erected a number of first-class houses in Railway Street, which are models in their way when compared with the cottages of fifty years or a century ago. He has now built several additional comfortable dwellings on the Glen Road, which will be a marked improvement to the locality.

And election fever was in the air, with a by-election for County Down following the death of the sitting member, James Sharman Crawford. William Drennan Andrews, the uncle of Thomas Andrews and a well-known

Robert Todd's housing development in Railway Street. Note Boyd's shop

judge residing in Dublin, stood as a tenant-right candidate against Lord Castlereagh of the Liberal Party. There was trouble at a meeting of Mr Andrews' supporters in Newtownards; some blamed it on 'the bludgeon men brought over from Comber in endeavouring to expel persons whom Mr Andrews' local committee believed to belong to the opposite party'.

Lord Castlereagh was the victor at the polls:

William Drennan Andrews
1832–1924

> On Saturday evening, after the declaration of the poll, Comber presented a lively aspect. Knots of persons were gathered at the various corners, many extolling the inestimable virtues of the successful candidate, whilst others sympathised with the less fortunate Mr Andrews, but generally speaking the result was favourably received … In the evening the town was patrolled with a fife and drum band, which was followed by a vast number testifying their appreciation of the choice of the county, and enthusiastic in behalf of Lord Castlereagh.

The Non-Subscribing Church were erecting a schoolhouse, and needed to raise funds:

> A Bazaar in connection with the Unitarian congregation, Comber, and intended to assist by procuring the funds required for the erection of a school-room, and the promotion of other important improvements, will be held on the congregational grounds, on Wednesday, the 17th of July. The bazaar will be formally opened by John Miller Esq., JP, at half-past eleven o'clock. Contributions are respectively requested. It is hoped that friends assisting with donations of work, will kindly send them forward in good time. Tickets of admission, one shilling; after six o'clock P.M., sixpence.

The International Order of Good Templars stood in the front line against the evil of drink. It was felt that Comber should be involved:

> On Tuesday 29th Oct., a deputation from the Newtownards District Lodge visited Comber, and held a meeting in the Orange Hall for the

purpose of re-organising the Exodus Lodge. Rev. John Harris, DD, presided; the other chairs being filled by Newtownards brethren. Notwithstanding the severity of the weather, there was a good attendance of new members, and the lodge was successfully instituted. After the election and installation of the officers, a vote of thanks was passed to Bro Harris and the other visitors and the lodge was closed in the usual manner. At the usual weekly meeting, on Tuesday evening 5th November, there were nine candidates for initiation; so that, although in the enemy's stronghold, the Exodus promises to be a success.

1879

World Events

- Britain fights the Zulu War in South Africa; heroic defence of Rorke's Drift.
- Shakespeare Memorial Theatre is opened at Stratford-upon-Avon.
- Over 100 people are killed in the Tay Bridge Railway disaster in Scotland.

A long-standing partnership was dissolved on 6th January when John Andrews, son of Isaac, bought out the shares of his cousins James and John in Comber's flour and corn mills. The day of flour-milling in Comber, however, was coming to an end, and over the next few years the firm of Isaac Andrews & Sons made the move to Belfast.

How is this for good neighbourliness?

> The friends and neighbours of Mrs McKee, of Cattogs, near Comber, having heard that her farm had not been sold, on Tuesday last assembled with sixty-one ploughs, and turned over in excellent style all the land she wanted ploughed this season. In the evening those who took part in the proceedings, and a few friends, were hospitably entertained by Mrs McKee. Such a mark of respect in the present busy season speaks well for the good feeling that exists between Mrs McKee and her numerous friends around Comber.

Comber Fair was always quite a boisterous occasion, being held four times a year. Two of these occasions were hiring fairs. One such was held on 7th April:

The attendance at this fair, held on Monday last, of farmers and farm-servants was as large as usual, but wages were a great deal lower than in former years, as farmers were unwilling to concede former rates, owing to the great depression in trade for the past year, and servants were unwilling to accept any reduction which averaged from 20 to 30 per cent. About mid-day rain commenced to fall, which had the effect of driving people into the public-houses, and the result was that rowdyism was indulged in to a greater extent than has been witnessed for several years past. In some instances four fights could have been seen going on at the same time, and the police, some of whom had been drafted in from Newtownards and other outlying stations to preserve order, had a most difficult part to play.

Flooding was a perennial problem in Comber, and in July the River Enler burst its banks at Bridge Street. One correspondent to the *Newtownards Chronicle* offered some advice:

> … could the flooding … be prevented or remedied? I think it could. The "Weir", or "Battery" (as it is commonly termed) which is erected at the mouth of the Comber River for the purpose of keeping up the water for the accommodation of the distilleries company is the sole cause, without doubt, of all the flooding which this portion of the town is subjected to. The weir in question is fully three feet above the level of the bed of the river, which causes the water to be fully three feet higher than it would be were the weir not in existence, and consequently the river so overflows its banks that the low-lying district near the river becomes submerged, and the houses inundated to a very great extent. Now, my suggestion is, that to prevent the recurrence of the flooding, the present existing weir should be removed, and a continuous line of sluices, the entire breadth of the river, or some such like contrivance substituted, to serve the twofold purpose of keeping up the water for the brewery, and of being capable of being opened when the waters assume their wonted and disastrous proportions.

First Comber congregation were shocked by the death of their minister since 1843, Rev. James M. Killen, on 3rd September:

> It is our melancholy duty today to announce the death of this well known minister, which occurred suddenly at Donaghadee on Wednesday evening. He had been staying with his family for some weeks at that favourite watering place. For a good many months he had occasional attacks of rheumatism, and it was known to himself and his friends that he was labouring under an affection of the heart,

from which, however, his medical advisors did not seem to apprehend any immediate danger. Though not strong, he continued very much in his usual health till the end of last week, but on Friday night and Saturday he was seriously indisposed. Failing to obtain a supply for his pulpit, he was obliged to preach in Comber on Sabbath last, and returned to Donaghadee on Monday ... the last words he was heard to whisper were "Christ is sufficient".

This meant that two of Comber's churches were temporarily without a minister, for on 11th May Rev. John Orr had resigned from his charge of the Non-Subscribing Church.

Football played in Comber in 1879 was of the oval ball variety, as evidenced by the match on 1st November between North Down F.C. and R.A. Institution:

> This match was played at Comber on Saturday last, and after a slight struggle, resulted in a victory for North Down by one goal and eight tries to nil. There was a good attendance of spectators, which shows that there is an increasing interest attached to this favourite recreation in this neighbourhood.

1880

World Events

- The Boers declare war on Britain and drive them out of the Transvaal.
- Gladstone's Liberal Party wins the General Election.
- Events in County Mayo lead to the first use of the term 'boycott'.
- The first London telephone directory has 255 names.
- The Irish Football Association is formed.
- Liverpool becomes a city.
- W.G. Grace scores 152 for England against Australia at the Oval.
- Death of the novelist George Eliot.

The new Non-Subscribing minister was installed on 27th January. This was Rev. Thomas Dunkerley, who came from a London congregation. The buildings were in shipshape condition for his arrival:

Interior of Non-Subscribing Church showing balcony of 1880

We should state that the new and beautiful schoolhouse has been completed, as also the gallery in the church, which will, of course, afford increased accommodation to the members. The manse, vestry rooms, and vestibule of the church have been renovated; and two dwelling-houses, with stabling accommodation in rear for the use of members of the congregation, are in course of erection at the entrance gate in Mill Street.

The total outlay was over £1,500, of which John Miller contributed £400.

First Comber's new minister was Rev. John McKeown, a licentiate of the Belfast Presbytery, ordained on 23rd March. It was stated that 'Mr McKeown enters the ministry on a full tide of Christian sympathy and goodwill'.

A well-known character was found dead on 6th March. An inquest was held into

… the death of Jane Browne, who was better known in the neighbourhood as "herrin' Sally". On Saturday, the deceased, who was about seventy years of age, was found dead in a small stream of water, in the townland of Carnesure. It is supposed she was gathering sticks and fell into the water and was drowned.

There was also a fatal accident at the Distillery on 8th July:

> James Dunn, known as "Steeple-Jack", was engaged executing some
> repairs to one of the chimneys, and when working at the top, portion
> of his supports gave way, and he was precipitated to the ground, a
> distance of seventy or eighty feet. He only survived some twenty
> minutes, having sustained terrible injuries.

An ornamental iron railing was to be erected in front of the Orange Hall.
An entertainment was arranged to raise funds:

> The first part was a lecture by the Rev. R.H. Coote, rector of
> Donaghadee, which was listened to with great attention by a large
> audience. It took the form of a narrative of his travels through
> Switzerland, France, and Italy, and he engaged the patient attention of
> his audience for nearly an hour and a half, being frequently applauded.
> The second part was a capital rendering by the Comber Church choir
> … under the direction of Mr A.H. De Wind.

There was always consternation when the rates increased. This happened at
the end of September, and Mr Ritchie asked the Poor Law Guardians why
Comber rates had gone up from 11 pence in the pound to one shilling and
two pence. It was explained that there was a charge of two pence for water
and sewerage on the town and townparks of Comber, the people who would
be using these facilities. There is nothing new under the sun.

A massive demonstration took place on 28th December:

> A tenant-right meeting, of a most enthusiastic character, was held on
> Monday evening in a large room of the Messrs Andrews' Spinning
> Mill, Comber. There was a very large attendance of tenant-farmers,
> the room being crowded almost to inconvenience in every part, nearly
> one thousand persons being present.

The object of the meeting was to whip up support for a new Land Bill, with
resolutions being passed in favour of farmer proprietary [ownership as
opposed to leasing from a landlord], and fixity of tenure, fair rents and free
sale. It was agreed that copies of the resolutions be forwarded to Mr
Gladstone, the prime minister.

1881

World Events

- After defeat by the Boers at Majuba Hill, Britain recognises the independence of Transvaal.
- The US President James Garfield is assassinated.
- Flogging is abolished in the British Army.
- The Irish National Land League is outlawed; Charles Stuart Parnell is arrested for active opposition to Gladstone's Land Act.
- Lord Salisbury is the new Conservative party leader, following the death of Disraeli.
- The Natural History Museum opens in Kensington, London.

One resident of Comber was concerned at the state of Comber's housing:

> What I complain of is the dilapidated appearance of house property. To a stranger, at first sight, Comber house property would seem to be in the hands of paupers, but on further inquiry he will discover it is not so, but quite the reverse. This makes him still more bewildered. Surely something might be done to remedy this shameful state of house property. I would suggest that a few of the leading owners, such as the Messrs Andrews, Allen, McConnell, McCance, and others, should set the example, and at once try to wipe off the disgrace to which Comber has had to submit for many years.

Tragedy occurred on 15th August at the Pound Bridge in Mill Street with the death of a seven-year-old boy called James McKenzie. John McMooran (aged 75) was brought up in court, charged by Constable Dunne with having caused his death:

> It appeared that on the day in question the accused was driving his daughter and two grandchildren to the railway station when the pony took fright at some children playing in Mill Street, and dashed off at a furious pace, which the defendant was unable to control. On passing the Pound Bridge the deceased, who had been getting a can of water, attempted to cross the road, but fell in the venture, and was run over, and died from the effects of the injuries in about three-quarters of an hour. The Coroner's jury, who held an inquest on the body, returned a verdict of accidental death.

Lower Distillery Dam with The Crescent in the background

Another accident involved Robert Blair of High Street, whose body was found early in the morning in the dam of the Lower Distillery [on the Newtownards Road]. An inquest was held:

> Thomas John Withers, MD, swore that he examined the body, and found no marks of violence. It was stiff and cold, and must have been in the water for six hours or more. It had the appearance of a man who fell into the water under the influence of drink.

A verdict of accidental drowning was returned, and the Distillery came in for some criticism because the dam was not properly fenced off.

First Comber had a debt to wipe out, and special sermons were preached on 4th September by the Moderator, Rev. W. Fleming Stevenson, to try to reduce this. Meanwhile, at Second Comber, the manse and schoolhouse were enlarged. And in the Erasmus Smith School in the Square a bazaar and fancy fair was held in October, the proceeds of which were devoted to the establishment of a coffee room in Comber. The room, with a reading room attached, opened in December in Mill Street.

'Boycott' was a relatively new word in the English language. Something close to a boycott almost occurred at Comber in December when the Distillery put up the price of grain sold by them to farmers:

On Thursday evening week an adjourned meeting of those interested in "distillery grains" was held … to consider the advisability of discontinuing the purchase of that commodity, in consequence of a recent advance of a penny per bushel by the Comber Distilleries Co. The farmers seem to be of one opinion – that any increase is not warranted, by the diminution in the prices of grain, which has been materially reduced in value here these past few days. It is a matter to cause sincere regret that the action of any party culminates in such illegality, as this meeting was originated solely to "Boycott" the grains. In this loyal division of Co. Down such practices should be entirely discountenanced, as we have it on the highest authority that all combinations tending to obstruct or interfere with the trader are illegal.

1882

World Events

- Charles Stuart Parnell is released from Kilmainham prison after a secret agreement to bring to an end violence over the Land Act.
- Cavendish and Burke are assassinated in Phoenix Park, Dublin.
- Charles Darwin dies.
- Gottlieb Daimler builds a petrol engine.
- The first hydro-electric plant starts to function in Wisconsin, USA.

An uncle of Thomas Andrews died on 7th February while on holiday in France. This was James Andrews of Carnesure (so called because he had built Carnesure House):

The deceased was one of those energetic merchants who have raised the North of Ireland to the proud position it occupies, and as principal partner in the eminent firms of John Andrews & Sons and James Andrews & Sons, he in a great measure tended to make the name of the firms world-wide. All his life, the late James Andrews was a financier, in which department he had few equals. It was the pleasure of his life to be controlling the

James Andrews of Carnesure 1829–82

books of which he had supervision, and success was ever the great object he had in view.

As well as his connection with the Andrews mills, James had been a magistrate, a director of the Belfast and County Down Railway, and treasurer of the Non-Subscribing Church in Comber. He was buried in the family vault in the churchyard of St Mary's.

No doubt Thomas would have taken part in the annual Sunday school fete in connection with the Non-Subscribing Church held in July:

> In the morning the children, with their teachers and friends, assembled in the school-room in Mill Street, and having been marshalled by the Rev. T. Dunkerley, proceeded to the railway station, where a train was in waiting to convey them to Newcastle … The party numbered about 200, with appropriate and tastefully designed banners, and the procession was headed by the Comber Flute Band, attired in handsome artillery uniform … On arriving at Newcastle the procession marched to the Sand Hills, where a pleasant day was spent in a most enjoyable manner …

1883

World Events

- Paul Kruger becomes President of the Transvaal.
- Karl Marx dies.
- The Boys' Brigade is founded.
- The Orient Express first runs.
- *Treasure Island* by Robert Louis Stevenson is published.
- Portrush is linked to Bushmills by the first electric tramway in Britain.
- The island of Krakatoa in Indonesia almost entirely disappears following a volcanic eruption.

One of Comber's most distinguished citizens passed away in January at the age of 87. John Miller had been born in Downpatrick and held a position in connection with the Customs before settling in Comber in 1826. At that time he became a partner in Comber Upper Distillery, later becoming sole

owner of both Distilleries, before
selling them to Samuel Bruce in
1871. John Miller was also
instrumental in establishing the
Non-Subscribing Church in
Comber, procuring the use of a
loft for early meetings before the
church was built on Windmill
Hill. The church benefited greatly
from his generosity. He was also a
magistrate, an ex-officio member
of the Newtownards Board of
Guardians, and one of the
directors of the Belfast and County
Down Railway. (Later in the year
Thomas Andrews of Ardara was
appointed to Mr Miller's vacant

John Miller 1796–1883

post as director of the BCDR). The funeral was to the graveyard of the Non-
Subscribing Church.

James Milling of the Square, who
owned one of Comber's oldest
businesses (established 1731),
marketed a new product:

Among the branches of business
recently established in the thriving
town of Comber is the
manufacture of aerated waters in
the Square by Mr James Milling,
who is always anxious in every way
to promote the welfare of the town
and district. The waters appear to
be of the best quality, and, as stated
on the label, none but the purest
ingredients appear to be used. The
label attached to each bottle is
neatly made up, and bears as a
trade mark the statue of General
Rollo Gillespie, which stands in
the centre of the Square. We have
no doubt the waters will be largely
patronised as local manufactures

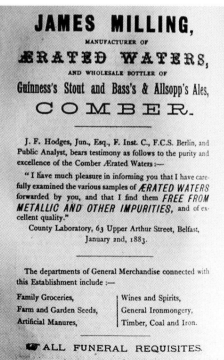

Milling's aerated waters – no household
should be without this refreshing drink

by the people of North Down. We can testify as to their purity and quality, and no household at this particular season should be without them.

William McCullough, a farm servant employed by James McCracken of Ballyrickard near Comber, died in a shooting accident:

> It appeared that on the 16th May a fellow-servant named Alexander Moore got a gun in his master's house for the purpose of shooting or "scaring" away crows, and, not knowing the gun was loaded, he put a fresh cap on, pulled the trigger, and the contents lodged in the head of McCullough, who was standing convenient to him.

There was another fatal accident near Comber in June:

> An accident by which a man named Macauley lost his life, took place on Saturday morning on the Ballywilliam Road, about half a mile from Comber. It appears that Macauley, who was servant to a farmer living a short distance out of Comber, was taking a number of young swine belonging to his master into town, when the horse bolted, and the deceased was thrown out of the cart. The wheel passed over his body, injuring him very severely. He was picked up a few minutes afterwards by a farmer who was passing, and taken into Comber, where Dr Withers attended to him. Medical skill was, however, of no avail, as he died within three hours from the time he received the injuries.

One of the largest pedigree herds of cattle came under the hammer at auction:

> Mr John Thornton will sell by auction on Wednesday, August 22nd, at Unicarville, one mile from Comber … the extensive herd of pure bred shorthorns belonging to George Allen Esq. Established thirty-six years ago it numbers over 80 head … Numerous prizes have been won with the stock at the Royal and North-East Shows.

Speeding is not just a modern-day phenomenon:

> John Glover, car-driver, Comber, was summoned by Sub-Constable Christopher Byrne for furiously driving a horse and car through the public street in Comber on the 22nd July. The constable stated one would have thought it was a steeplechase he was running, he was going at such a furious rate.

Isaac Andrews died in September. He was an uncle of Thomas Andrews' father:

Isaac Andrews 1799–1883

> The funeral of Mr Isaac Andrews took place on Monday morning at half-past eleven o'clock, and was attended by a large circle of personal friends of the deceased. The remains were interred in the family burying-ground, Comber. The deceased ... died, widely respected, on Thursday week, at the great age of eighty-four years. Until within the past year he enjoyed excellent health, and though latterly feeble, he died in the full possession of all his faculties. Mr Andrews was one of the principal partners in Comber Flour Mills, in which he is succeeded by his sons, Messrs T. J. Andrews and John Andrews.

His sons shortly afterwards took the decision to close the Comber Flour Mill and move the entire operation to Belfast.

Thomas Andrews had another brother on 26 December. However, tragedy struck when this child died on 27th January 1884.

1884

World Events

- The Circle Line is completed on the London Underground system.
- Women are allowed to compete in the Lawn Tennis championships at Wimbledon.
- The Maxim machine gun is invented.
- A Reform Act gives the vote to every householder in Britain with property worth more than £10 a year.

There was a proposal to link Comber to Killyleagh via a tramway:

> On Tuesday evening [4th March] a meeting of the inhabitants of Comber and the surrounding district who are opposed to being taxed in support of this tramway was held in the Spinning Mill Schoolroom, Comber. There was a large attendance, the commodious room being filled to overflowing by the cesspayers of the neighbourhood.

After much discussion, a petition against the project was signed by those present and forwarded to the Grand Jury of County Down. Nothing ever came of the tramway.

Dogs and corner boys were the chief sources of annoyance to one Comber resident:

> The first nuisance and inconvenience to the public comfort and safety is the large number of dogs permitted to roam through the streets without let or hindrance. I am at a loss to know why people keep dogs when they have no use for them. The dogs kept at large are a positive danger to pedestrians, cattle, and horses, besides they are a nuisance on the streets, where they are encouraged by "corner idlers" to a continual process of fighting. A farmer from the country cannot pass through the streets with his dog in charge without being set upon by the corner idlers and their dogs. Against this there is no protection by any visible authority. The second nuisance and inconvenience to public comfort and convenience is the large number of corner-boys who are permitted without the least interference to occupy the entire footway against all other pedestrians. There is surely an unpardonable neglect of duty somewhere when the rowdyism of Comber corners is permitted to run so rampant that a female cannot be allowed to pass without being subjected to the low, vulgar taunts and blackguard expressions of an

uncontrolled rabble. Then again, there is the profane swearing by all
the attributes of the Deity, which should be brought under the notice
of the magistracy by the police.

Not a rioter in sight in this peaceful snapshot of Comber station

However, the corner boy problem was a storm in a teacup compared with
the riot at Comber Railway Station on Easter Monday. The disturbance was
caused by a group of bandsmen who were trying to get into the guard's brake
van of the train. John Medley, manager of the railway, and James Pinion,
traffic superintendent, attempted to stop them, whereupon they were
attacked by the mob. Mr Medley received a blow on the head, before
managing to escape on to the buffers, where he was hit on the head by a
lemonade bottle. Mr John Andrews of Knock tried to go to the assistance of
Mr Pinion, but was attacked by the crowd, who were brandishing leather
belts. He managed to fight his way through to the booking office. Later Mr
Pinion was led into the office half fainting.

A well known Comber doctor passed away in May:

> It is with sincere regret and yet with feelings of relief that we record the
> death of Dr James Frame, who had been suffering for some time past
> from a malady that was known to the inhabitants of Comber to be
> incurable ... Dr Frame, who was in his 74th year, was born near
> Comber ... and there commenced his practice as a surgeon ... He ...
> discharged his duties conscientiously, and amongst the poor his death
> will be severely felt ...

Dr Robert Henry

Dr Robert Henry succeeded him as medical officer of the Comber Dispensary, not without protest from Dr Withers, the unsuccessful candidate.

At a general meeting of the brethren of the Loyal Orange Lodges of Comber, held in the Orange and Protestant Hall on Saturday, it was unanimously agreed to hold a great demonstration to celebrate the anniversary of the Battle of the Boyne on the coming Twelfth of July in a field immediately adjoining the town, on the leading road to Newtownards, kindly granted for the occasion by George Allen Esq, of Unicarville.

Arches were erected in Mill Street, Bridge Street, High Street and Crescent Row, with a beautiful floral arch at the entrance to the field. An estimated 6,000 people attended, with lodges from Comber being joined by those from Newtownards, Bangor and the Ards Peninsula. Unfortunately the day was marred by the death of an Orangeman as some of the lodges made their way home out the Killinchy Road. A quarrel arose between Alex Houston of Ardmillan and Thomas Buckley of Ravarnett, during which Houston was knocked down by a blow from his adversary and never recovered. Buckley was said to be under the influence of drink.

A Neolithic discovery was made at Ballyloughan in the field of John Glover:

> We dug out carefully an urn containing human remains, which had been partially cremated, together with four worked flint flakes of the leaf type. In the same field two other urns were discovered by the occupier; one is at present in the hands of Mr Glover; the other is in the possession of S. Stone Esq., JP. Mr Stone's urn is an ornamental one, and I believe also contained human remains; Glover's is a plain urn, apparently well baked, and stands about nine inches high. It contained no bones, but was provided with a large heavy stone lid ...

Thomas Andrews became a pupil at Royal Belfast Academical Institution (Inst) in September 1884. Up until then he had been tutored privately.

Island Hill was the surprise venue for a major event on Comber's sporting calendar:

> The regatta was held for the first time on Saturday last [20th September] at Island Hill, near Comber. This regatta had been in

Island Hill with causeway submerged

contemplation for some time past, as the bay in which it was held is beautifully situated, and affords plenty of space for racing of the nature entered into, and by way of experiment two races were engaged in, the result being highly satisfactory. At the time announced for the first race the Hill, from which a splendid view can be obtained for miles around, and the immediate vicinity were crowded with spectators. The Comber Flute Band was in attendance, and played a variety of popular airs during the day. The weather was fine, the sun shining almost all day, and a bracing wind, at times light and variable, blowing south-west. The commodore, Mr John Murray, the secretary, Mr Samuel McKeown, and treasurer, Mr James Simpson, and committee are deserving of every credit for the successful manner in which the arrangements were carried out.

Proceedings ended with a duck hunt, in which 'Mr Thomas Hiles performed the part of duck in such a way as to give his pursuers plenty of trouble before securing him'.

The County Down election was won by the Conservative candidate:

Comber had its rejoicings in a most enthusiastic manner. Tar-barrels were burned, and the splendid Comber Flute Band paraded the streets playing appropriate airs in honour of the victorious return of ... Captain Ker.

1885

World Events

- General Charles Gordon is killed at Khartoum in the Sudan by the forces of the Mahdi.
- Lord Salisbury becomes Prime Minister.
- Gladstone declares himself to be in favour of Home Rule for Ireland.
- *The Mikado* is the latest hit production of Gilbert and Sullivan.
- Sir H. Rider Haggard writes *King Solomon's Mines*.
- Karl Benz builds his first motor car – a three wheeler.

There was concern about the state of Comber graveyard at St Mary's Church:

> ... the committee [Newtownards Board of Guardians] agreed with the report of Dr Henry, the dispensary doctor, that the extension of the present graveyard was necessary, and recommended that the Board of Guardians communicate with the Church Temporalities Commissioners as to the best means of enlarging the present graveyard, and the committee highly approved of the taking in of adjoining ground.

It was observed that some recent interments had only a few inches of soil over the coffins. There was a proposal to procure a new burial ground at the Glassmoss, but this appears to have been unacceptable to many because it was too far out of Comber, and there were numerous petitions against it. An alternative suggestion was Mr Corbitt's field on the Newtownards Road, much nearer the town.

The Comber sewerage system, or rather lack of it, was also coming in for criticism:

> Mr John Andrews JP said it was hardly creditable in the town of Comber, with a population of two thousand inhabitants, which was increasing, that there was no main sewer in it. Of course there was a sewer running through the town for the purpose of carrying off the surface water, but no person had any right to empty any sewerage matter into it ... No doubt if a proper sewerage scheme was laid out it would cost some money, but opposite that would be the result in the case of an epidemic breaking out in the town. To use the words of the dispensary medical officer, that in case of cholera – which was again

threatened this season – Comber would be a "pest-hole". The consequence would be dreadful – all the mills would have to be closed, and this would throw an immense number of the population on the rates to be supported, which would be a serious matter.

Castle Espie auction notice

The Castle Espie lime, brick, tile and pottery works came up for auction on 6th November. These works had closed in 1879 following the death of the owner Samuel Murland the previous year. The new owners were the Craig family of Tyrella.

First Comber's minister received a call to a congregation in England:

> Comber Presbytery met on Tuesday ... A call from the New John Street Congregation, Birmingham, to the Rev. John McKeown MA, Comber ... was submitted ... Mr Patrick McKeag and Mr John Adair, elders of First Comber, pleaded for his retention on the grounds that he was very much esteemed by the congregation, and that his pastoral labours were increasingly useful ... Mr McKeown addressed the Court, referring to the friendly and pleasant character of his relations to the congregation and Presbytery, regretting for several reasons leaving his present field of labour, and saying that he had decided to accept the call, with the sanction of the Presbytery.

1886

World Events

- Gladstone, back in power, is defeated over Home Rule.
- The foundation stone of Tower Bridge is laid in London.
- Britain annexes the kingdom of Upper Burma.
- Robert Louis Stevenson writes *Dr Jekyll and Mr Hyde*.
- The Severn Tunnel is opened.
- The Canadian Pacific Railway is completed.

A large loyalist demonstration took place in the Orange Hall in February, the main purpose of which was to protest against the proposed Home Rule Bill of Mr Gladstone, the Liberal Prime Minister. When the Bill was defeated in June, Comber celebrated:

> Liberals and Conservatives were equally enthusiastic. The Messrs Andrews, who are well known and consistent Liberals, and the largest employers in the town or in this neighbourhood, who are highly and deservedly respected by all classes of the community, entered heartily into the rejoicings. Bonfires were lighted, and the general congratulations were of the most jubilant character. The loyal town of Comber showed unmistakable tokens on this eventful evening of their unalloyed attachment to our gracious Queen and glorious Constitution.

First Comber finally got their new minister in August after being earlier turned down by Rev. Robert Smythe of Castleblayney. The new man was Robert Hanna, formerly minister in Croydon. These were momentous times for the congregation, for major renovation work had to be carried out on the church:

> A special closing service was held in this church on 26th Sept 1886 by the Rev. Dr Magill of Cork, Ex-Moderator of the General Assembly, on the occasion of closing the church for extensive alterations and repairs. There was a large attendance of the members and friends. At the close of a very earnest address a collection was taken up in aid of the renovation fund. The total amount realised from all sources amounted to £100.

There was a tragedy just outside Comber in June:

> Dr Parke JP, County Coroner for the Northern Division of Down, held an inquest on Saturday at Ballyrickard ... on the body of William John Orr, an extensive farmer, who committed suicide by hanging on the previous day. The family of the deceased are amongst the most respectable in the neighbourhood, and the sad occurrence has cast a gloom over the whole district ... The evidence showed that the deceased was in a very depressed state of mind ...

Thomas Andrews' youngest brother was born on 25th August. This was Willie, who grew up to be very well known in cricketing circles.

Comber Fair Day on 19th October was quite an occasion, resulting in several individuals appearing in Court:

> Sergeant Kirley deposed that ... the defendant Steele was drunk and disorderly in Comber. The proceedings of the defendant led to a row, which might have developed into a serious riot. The police, when engaged with this man, were assaulted by another man, the defendant David White. Stones were thrown at them by a large crowd, and very violent language was used. The police, however, succeeded in arresting White and in taking him to the barracks. The mob numbered perhaps 4,000 or 5,000 people. [surely a gross exaggeration]. The police were not injured by the stones, as none of them struck them. White afterwards maliciously broke some things in the strong room of the barracks which would take about 5s to repair. Constable Willis deposed to the arrest of John Steele, and to David White coming forward and striking Constable Sharpe on the face, knocking off his helmet.

George Allen of Unicarval died on 17th November:

> The melancholy event was very sudden and unexpected. It was only on Thursday week that he occupied a seat on the bench at the Petty Sessions ... it was chiefly as an agriculturalist he was known, not only throughout the County Down, but throughout the Three Kingdoms. In the breeding of high-class cattle, Mr Allen attained a celebrity second to none. His herds of Shorthorns were of the purest strains, and were much sought after by the best judges; and the sales at Unicarval attracted buyers from far beyond the limits of this county.

The streets were being neglected:

> Attention has been drawn to the disgraceful state of the streets of
> Comber. Certainly there is great room for complaint in regard to this
> matter, as even during this week the amount of accumulated dirt and
> slush in the leading street from the railway station to the Square was
> really astonishing.

It seems that much of the burden of cleaning was falling on one poor man:
'One man, it seems, has no less of road to clean and scrape than from the
railway station up to a couple of miles on the Killinchy Road'.

At least the railway station was neat and tidy, and received a first prize
award from the Belfast and County Down Railway for its 'very tasteful
horticultural and gardening ornamentation'.

1887

World Events

- Charles Stuart Parnell is accused of complicity in the Phoenix Park
  murders.
- Queen Victoria celebrates her golden jubilee.
- The character of Sherlock Holmes first appears in *A Study in Scarlet*
  by Arthur Conan Doyle.
- An electric lamp is produced for domestic use.
- Daimler 4-wheeled motor car produced.

A well-known character bowed out of Comber's public affairs:

> We exceedingly regret that, in consequence of failing health, Mr James
> Brownlow JP, who for upwards of twenty-two years has been agent for
> the Marquis of Londonderry, has felt himself obliged to resign his
> official position. He is succeeded by his son, Mr Charles Brownlow,
> who has lately been assisting his father in the management of the
> property ...

Brownlow Street in Comber is named in this gentleman's honour.

There was a horrific tragedy on 12th February:

> On Saturday night last an old woman named Jane
> McKee, 72 years of age, who resided in Bridge
> Street, Comber, received such serious injuries
> from burns accidentally contracted that she died
> on Sunday morning. It appears that about eleven
> o'clock on Saturday night she got out of bed to
> light a candle, when the lighted match
> accidentally caught her nightdress, and she was
> immediately surrounded in flames. Her son-in-
> law went to her assistance, and afterwards for Dr
> Wallace, but the injuries were so serious that she
> died about four o'clock on Sunday morning.

Before the renovations –
1st Comber with outside
steps and balcony

First Comber Church re-opened on 20th March
following the renovations:

> The re-opening services, after restoration, were held in First Comber
> Church by the Rev. John MacDermott, Belfast, on Sunday last ... The
> roof, galleries, flooring, and pews have been removed, and the interior
> reconstructed in an ingenious and suitable manner ... The entire
> church has been reseated with pews of modern style, matching in
> design and colour the treatment of the ceiling ... The general
> arrangement of the windows and the additional gables have given the

After the renovations at 1st Comber. Note the battlemented wall

old house quite a new appearance. The grounds have been tastefully laid out in terrace fashion and planted with choice shrubs, under the supervision of Messrs A. Dickson & Sons, Newtownards. The boundary walls are ornamented with battlements, and at the immediate front next the street are a pair of very handsome entrance gates, with railings, and also an upper gate leading to the school ... It was pleasant to observe the good fellowship existing between the different ministers of Comber on Sunday last, the Rev. D.A. Taylor, 2nd Comber, being among those present at the re-opening services.

There was also work to be done at Second Comber, and in May tenders were being sought for the erection of a schoolmaster's residence. Unfortunately, the congregation lost one of its most influential members:

It is with feelings of the most sincere regret that we announce the death of Mr John McConnell JP, which took place on Sunday evening last at Portrush, where he had been visiting. Mr McConnell had been in delicate health for some time, but his death came upon his friends as a painful surprise. He was head of the firm of Messrs J. & J. McConnell & Co. Ltd, Belfast, and was distinguished for honour and integrity in all his commercial relationships.

The Golden Jubilee of Queen Victoria fell in June 1887:

In Comber the Jubilee was recognised in a loyal manner. Flags floated over the Messrs Andrews' mill and the houses of the following: – James Davidson Esq., Carnesure House, A.H. De Wind Esq., CE, R. Henry MD, the Police Barrack, and the one over the top of First Comber Presbyterian Church, which consisted of a Union Jack, with a profile of her Majesty in the centre, on account of the height, was seen for miles around. The Sabbath-schools in connection with First Presbyterian Church made the day an annual excursion by proceeding to Ballygraffin. Nearly every person in Comber accompanied the children to Mr and Mrs John Adair's, where sports were indulged in during the day.

There were further celebrations in August when North Down Cricket Club won the first ever Senior Challenge Cup final when they beat North of Ireland at Ormeau by an innings and 5 runs. The team was captained by John Andrews Junior. What a day that must have been for the young Thomas Andrews, who by this time was a member of the club, making his first appearance on the team at the tender age of 14. Was he at the final as a spectator?

Victorious North Down team of 1887 (to the left of the Cup)

1888

World Events

- Jack the Ripper terrorises London.
- Keir Hardie founds the Scottish Labour Party.
- The English Football League is formed.
- Elected County Councils are established in England and Wales.
- Wilhelm II becomes Kaiser (Emperor) of Germany.
- J.B. Dunlop invents the pneumatic tyre.
- Vincent Van Gogh paints *Sunflowers*.

The schoolmaster's residence at Second Comber was completed at a cost of £250. The master, Mr Macrory,

> agreed to occupy the residence as long as he continued principal of Smyth's National School, under an annual rent of £6 5s 0d, being the

interest of the money borrowed from the government. He also agreed to take the adjoining field at a rent of £1 and to pay cess and taxes.

Another of Comber's schoolmasters could not take any more of it:

> About ten o'clock on Tuesday morning Mr Alex Stewart, school-teacher, attempted to commit suicide at his lodgings, Mr Riddell's, High Street. He was well-known and generally respected as the head teacher of the Mill Schools in connection with Messrs Andrews' extensive establishment. He had been noticed to be in a despondent state of mind for some time, and when in the breakfast-room on Tuesday morning he suddenly lifted a table knife and inflicted a gash in his throat. An alarm was given, and Sergeant Kirley of the Comber police was on the spot immediately. He called in Dr Henry and Dr Wallace, and when, on medical authority, it was stated that Mr Stewart was likely to recover there was great satisfaction.

There were major problems at First Comber:

> It is very seldom that so painful a case as that of the Rev. Robert Hanna, of Comber, has engaged the attention of the General Assembly ... Mr Hanna had been deposed by the Comber Presbytery; the Synod of Belfast altered this finding to a sentence of suspension. Against this an appeal was taken, and the Assembly, by a vote of 87 to 16, sustained the appeal, reversed the sentence of suspension imposed by the Synod, and confirmed that of deposition passed by the Presbytery of Comber. The Moderator then pronounced the sentence of deposition and degradation upon Mr Hanna.

Rev. Hanna's successor was Rev. T.S. Graham, formerly of Lisbellaw, installed on 30th October.

On 5th December the body of John McKeag was found in the mill pond. At the inquest:

> Alexander Thompson ... deposed that he saw deceased, who was 82 years of age, near the dam, and ten minutes afterwards he heard the alarm that a man was drowned. He went and helped to pull out the body ... The probability was that deceased had taken a weak turn, as he was liable to them, and had fallen into the water.

Rev. Thomas S. Graham (installed as minister of 1st Comber in 1888) with his family

1889

World Events

- The Eiffel Tower is completed in Paris.
- The Kodak camera comes into production, using photographic film.
- London trade is brought to a halt by a dock strike.
- J.K. Jerome published *Three Men in a Boat*.

Second Comber congregation celebrated its golden jubilee on 27th March, fifty years to the day after the laying of the foundation stone of the church:

> The proceedings took the form of a social meeting, which was most successful. There was a large attendance of members of the congregation and their friends. After tea an adjournment was made to the church, where the business part of the proceedings was carried out ...The meeting having been opened with prayer and praise, Rev. Mr Taylor, who presided, said it had fallen to his lot to give them that evening a history of the Second Comber Congregation.

Mr Taylor referred to 'the tempest that swept over the congregation' in the days of Rev. Rogers, concerned with a case of double-jobbing, as minister of Second Comber and as Professor of Sacred Rhetoric at Assembly's College, Belfast, and of the strong feelings when voting for his successor. But now:

> A spirit of harmony prevails ... During the past eleven years the membership has increased by one-third, the stipend payers by one-fourth, the average attendance at Sabbath-school has almost doubled, and many organisations, including the weekly prayer meeting, evangelistic efforts, temperance societies, district meetings, Dorcas, Zeuana, Orphan societies, have been formed which display a great amount of vitality. In regard to church buildings we have in ten years doubled the schoolroom, enlarged the manse, erected a handsome pulpit, made a new session-room, added to the accommodation for the comfort of the school children, formed a congregational library, supplied a heating apparatus, sunk a new well for the manse, built a schoolmaster's residence, and just now we are completing the whole establishment by erecting stables for the horses on Sabbath day ... Mr Wm McKee then presented to the Rev. Mr Taylor a handsome cassock and gown on behalf of the ladies of the congregation. He wished that Rev. Mr Taylor would be long spared to minister amongst them ...

There was also an address from the Moderator of the General Assembly.

Thomas Andrews left school at Inst in May at the age of 16, and became an apprentice at Harland and Wolff's shipyard, of which his mother's brother William James Pirrie was managing director. He moved into 'digs' in Belfast at this time.

In December Rev. George Smith of St Mary's became a canon when he was installed in Downpatrick Cathedral as rector of St Andrews, a church which no longer existed.

James Hamilton of Comber died on 27th December, after falling off a car the previous day about a mile outside Newtownards.

> The wheel of the car went over the lower part of his head and face. Dr McIlroy, Newtownards, Dr Henry, and Dr Wallace, Comber, were as soon as possible in attendance on the injured man, who, after great suffering from his severe injuries, died yesterday morning at four o'clock.

1890

World Events

- The first electric power station is opened at Deptford.
- Bismarck is dismissed as German chancellor.
- Cecil Rhodes becomes premier of Cape Colony.
- Charles Stuart Parnell resigns as leader of the Irish National Party.
- The Forth Bridge is completed.
- Moving picture films shown in New York.

At a time when typhoid fever was prevalent in the town, Dr Henry, the Comber Dispensary District medical officer reported that 80% of the houses in Comber had neither 'privies nor ashpit accommodations', and he recommended that steps be taken to remedy this state of things. The Crescent in particular was in a filthy state:

> Most of the people of Comber had been complaining at one time or another of the state of the sewers and asking him could nothing be done. People living beside the gratings had to place logs covered with sods over them in the summer, so as to be able to stay in their houses, and where that was not done the people passing had to cover their noses to keep off the offensive smell.

Notices had to be erected by the Board of Guardians 'warning people against throwing slops and night soil on the streets'.

The first point-to point steeplechase was held at Mount Alexander on 5th April:

> The course, which was a very stiff one, was about four miles in length ... There was a large and fashionable gathering of spectators, but undoubtedly the attendance would have been much greater if it had not been for counter-attractions elsewhere. This class of sport which has only recently been inaugurated in the country has rapidly become very popular, and we are sure if it is continued next season will prove a great source of enjoyment and pleasure to many. The competitions today were between teams of six, each representing the County Down Staghounds and the North Down Harriers ... The North Down won by 39 points to 38. The proceedings concluded with a drag hunt.

Woods' drapers' shop in Castle Street

In May there was a serious fire in Castle Street:

> The premises are situated immediately opposite the constabulary
> barracks, and are occupied by Mr Samuel Woods, who carries on the
> business of a draper. The fire was observed about nine o'clock in the
> evening. At that time there were several flashes of lightning, to which
> has been attributed the origin of the fire. The premises were gutted,
> and the damages are estimated to be about £200.

Who would be a schoolteacher?

> Miss Georgina Neill, school teacher, Comber, summoned Mrs Ellen
> Skillen ... for assault on the 14th May. The defendant's child was a pupil
> at complainant's school, and having received some chastisement from
> her teacher, her mother, the defendant, as alleged, assaulted Miss Neill.

There were scandalous goings-on at Island Hill:

> Ringcreevy, or The Island Hill, is the only suitable bathing-place for
> ladies in this district. Would you believe that men, who I am sure call
> themselves gentlemen, come when we are bathing, undress within a
> few yards of us, and, without any bathing costume, intrude on our
> bathing place? We do not know what to do except to give up bathing,
> which appears hard.

Robert Milligan of McConnells' Row [now sometimes called Todd's Row on the Belfast Road] was killed in November in an accident at Mr Blakely Orr's mill at Ballystockart:

> About half-past one o'clock on Monday a portion of flax got entangled in the rollers. Hamilton McDowell, roller-man, stopped the roller and cut it off, but deceased, it is believed, in an endeavour to get the flax out of the rollers, got caught in the machinery.

1891
World Events
- Factory Act – no child in Britain under the age of eleven is to work in a factory.
- An Act gives free education to all in England and Wales.
- Thomas Hardy publishes *Tess of the D'Urbervilles*.
- Newsagent and politician W.H. Smith dies.
- Keir Hardie is elected as an Independent Labour MP.

Improvements were being made at Comber Railway Station:

> The down platform to Belfast when finished will be almost double in length. This was necessary when three trains were frequently in the station at the same time.

Comber's platforms became the longest on the entire BCDR system at 832 feet.

About 5,000 people were in Comber for the Twelfth, held in the field of Thomas Horner at Mount Alexander. Lodges present were from the districts of Comber, Newtownards and Saintfield. Orange lilies decorated the houses and street lamps, and an arch of orange lilies adorned the entrance to the road leading to the place of meeting. The weather was glorious. Six extra constabulary were drafted in from County Meath, but no trouble is recorded.

1892

World Events

- Huge anti-Home Rule Convention is held in Belfast.
- Gladstone becomes Prime Minister for a fourth term.
- Toulouse-Lautrec paints *At the Moulin Rouge*.
- Alfred Lord Tennyson dies.
- Gold discovered in Western Australia.
- Major earthquake disaster in California.

A robbery took place during the evening service at Second Comber on 24th January. Overcoats, shawls and other articles belonging to John Ritchie were stolen from a trap which he had left in the stables. William Rogan subsequently confessed to the crime and was sentenced to a month in jail with hard labour.

These were trying times for Second Comber. In March their treasurer, Mr J.W. Ritchie, resigned:

> ... At a conference of the Belfast Presbytery it was resolved to "urge on all Christians the duty of excluding from offices in the Church all persons who are directly, or even by investment, connected with the drink traffic". Mr Ritchie... says he feels the resolution comes directly home to himself, and that he in consequence has resigned the office of treasurer of Second Comber, which he has held for sixteen years ...

There was tragedy at Island Hill on 30th April:

> On Saturday evening last, a melancholy occurrence took place near Comber, at a place called Island-hill ... resulting in the death by drowning of a boy named Wm J. McMillan, eleven years of age, who lived in Comber. Deceased and three boys, named Murdoch, Fisher, and Smyth, were gathering shellfish on the strand of the lough. They were crossing the strand at Castle Espie, and were surrounded by the tide, and were struggling for their lives, when three of them were rescued by a boy named John Bowman with a boat. The fourth boy (McMillan) was drowned.

This was the year of the great Ulster Unionist Convention in Belfast, one of the chief organisers being Thomas Andrews' father, Thomas of Ardara. A large meeting was held on 25th May at Comber Spinning Mill covering the

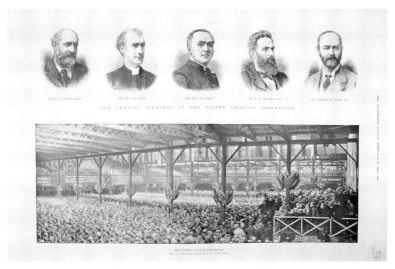

The Ulster Unionist Convention of 1892

Comber and Moneyrea polling districts to appoint delegates to attend and to protest against any attempt to force Home Rule on the people of Ulster:

> Rev. D.A. Taylor [minister of Second Comber], who was received with great enthusiasm, moved – 'That this meeting cordially approves of the objects of the great Convention to be held in Belfast on the 17th of June, and the resolutions to be proposed thereat, and pledges itself to use every effort to make the delegate meeting and the monster meeting in the Botanic Gardens a great success' ... They had been accused by Englishmen with being indifferent to this question of Home Rule. Because they had not been protesting and parading their threats it was concluded that they really did not care much about the matter ... if England had found it hard to quell Southern rebellion, she would find it a still tougher piece of business to meet the cool, determined, dogged, persevering purpose of the North, which would never submit to be dominated by a Home Rule Parliament, meeting in Dublin.

Other speakers included Thomas Andrews senior himself, Rev. Dr Graham of First Comber and Rev. Dunkerley of the Non-Subscribing Church.

A serious fire occurred in the stackyard of Mr H.E. Andrews of Carnesure:

> Fortunately help was at hand and about sixty hands from the Spinning Mill were soon on the spot and extinguished the flames. Even so, the greater part of a large stack worth about £30 was destroyed.

1893

World Events

- Statue of Eros unveiled in Piccadilly Circus, London.
- The Second Home Rule Bill is defeated in the House of Lords.
- Britain's first Ladies' Golf Championship is held.
- Manchester Ship Canal completed.
- Karl Benz produces a car with four wheels.
- Aspirin is first produced.

It was reported on 4th March that:

> On Friday evening last some heartless person left a female child, about three months old, behind the door of a farmer at Ballymaleddy, near Comber, when the people of the house were out milking. The infant was brought to Newtownards Workhouse on Saturday afternoon, and is still there.

The Home Rule issue was back on the agenda:

> On Saturday evening [11th March] a meeting of the Unionists of Comber and the adjoining districts was held in the roughing-room of Messrs Andrews's spinning mills to protest against the Home Rule Bill. The room, which is a commodious apartment, was filled to its utmost capacity, the attendance numbering considerably over a thousand people. There was a large number of ladies present. At the back of the platform the Union Jack was conspicuously displayed. The Chairman [Mr John Andrews JP, uncle of Thomas Andrews Junior] ... said they were assembled that evening to protest against the most infamous and nefarious Bill that ever had been tried to be foisted on a free country ... They (the Loyalists) did not want Home Rule, but if they were to choose between Home Rule as set forth in this Bill and total separation they would accept the latter ...

It was agreed to petition Parliament against the Bill.

Some people were prepared to use coercion of a different kind to get their way. A crowd attacked the house of Patrick Morgan, a Catholic living at Cattogs, threatening to kill him if he did not give his vote against Home Rule. Volleys of stones were thrown on the roof and the stable doors were kicked, resulting in frightened horses breaking loose and a valuable animal being lamed. The mob returned a few nights later, but following information received, the police were concealed in an outhouse. On this occasion they arrested David Patton of Castle Espie and John Douglas of Lisbarnett who put up a violent resistance.

A meeting was held on 15th April in the house of Mr T.J. Andrews of the Square [a cousin of Thomas Andrews' father] 'to discuss the establishing of a trained district nurse'. The Marchioness of Londonderry spoke of the work she had been involved in over in England, where they had formed a local nursing society. Another speaker was 'Miss Belle MacPherson, for so many years connected with, and lady superintendent of the Belfast Society for Providing Nurses for the Sick Poor, [who] then gave a most interesting description of the good work done in Belfast'.

> Dr R. Henry ... spoke of the great need of trained nursing in Comber ... This gentleman has from the first interested himself very heartily in the project, and his assistance and support are of inestimable value to the society ... The Rev. D. Taylor [said that] ... during his fifteen years of ministry in Comber he had often been struck with the great kindness of the poor to one another, but there were, of course, many cases where not only neighbourly kindness, but professional knowledge was necessary in order to be of use to the sick, and he believed a trained nurse would supply this want.

And so Comber Nursing Society was formed, and later in the year Nurse Fenton was appointed as District Nurse.

Completion of a major project on the railway was announced on 3rd June:

> The doubling of the railway line from Knock to Comber, about five miles, has been finished, and there is now an up-line and a down-line from Belfast to Comber junction, eight miles ... A large number of trains had formerly to stop at Knock till trains coming on the opposite direction would pass.

But a further scheme came to nought:

> A project has been mooted in some of the Belfast papers of making a line of railway from Killyleagh, through Killinchy to Comber; and it is suggested, in connection therewith, that a steamer should be placed on Strangford Lough to run between Portaferry and Killyleagh. This we consider a very utopian scheme. Killyleagh and Killinchy are each within a few miles of the present railway system, and the prospects of

a new line in that district are not to be compared with the prospects of a line through the Ards.

Up until this time, one of the tablets on the Gillespie Monument had remained blank. It was now decided that this should be rectified by inscribing a memorial to another Major-General Robert Rollo Gillespie. This was a grandson of the man on the statue who had also served in India and died in 1890 in command of the Mhow Division of the Bengal Army.

1894

World Events

- Blackpool Tower is opened.
- Gladstone is succeeded as Prime Minister by the Earl of Roseberry.
- Rudyard Kipling writes *The Jungle Book*.
- Uganda becomes a British Protectorate.
- Alfred Dreyfus is convicted in France on a treason charge and imprisoned on Devil's Island.
- Louis Lumiere invents the cinematograph.

A sewerage scheme for Comber eventually went ahead, despite opposition from some who did not like the idea of having to pay for it. The sum of £1,000 was being borrowed and that would be added on to the rates. But there can be no doubt that the work was badly needed. The stench was apparently dreadful, especially during hot weather, and John Andrews had himself covered over some of the gratings in an attempt to keep the smell down.

And, after years of discussion and negotiation, Comber at last got its new cemetery on the Newtownards Road, the first burial being Mrs Martha McDowell of Troopersfield. But already, in January, the vandals had been at work and 'injuries had been maliciously done to the gate and railings'. Some of the workmanship was deemed to be inferior, especially the wall, and the entrance was not built according to the plans. Nevertheless in April Comber Burial Committee expressed approval of the manner in which Messrs Alex Dickson & Sons had laid out and planted the grounds. John W. Ritchie had

Comber Cemetery, opened 1894

been appointed secretary to the Committee at £25 a year. David Parker of Newtownards got the job of caretaker of the cemetery at 14s a week wages with free house and garden.

Francis Munn, the stationmaster, left Comber on May on his promotion to Downpatrick:

> Your many friends in Comber cannot allow your departure to take place without some expression of the general regret that exists, and without testifying in some way to their appreciation of the admirable way in which you have discharged the duties of the arduous and onerous post which you have occupied here for the past ten years. At all times we have seen you attentive to your duty, ready, firm, and obliging. We recognise that in a great degree the regularity and smoothness of the traffic at our station has been due to your active watchfulness, sound judgement, and business capacity ... As the outcome of spontaneous feeling and the work of ready hands voicing the expression of willing hearts, we beg your acceptance of the accompanying clock, ornaments, and purse of sovereigns.

Thomas Andrews' five year apprenticeship at Harland and Wolff's came to an end. For the past eighteen months he had found his true vocation, as a junior member of the drawing office team.

The year ended on a sad note:

> On Monday Mr James Shields, one of the oldest and most respected inhabitants of Comber, committed suicide. It appears that on a member of the family going to an outhouse in the morning he discovered to his great horror the deceased hanging lifeless, suspended by a rope round his neck. For fully a quarter of a century the deceased held an important position in connection with the local distilleries. Failing intellect, coupled with the infirmities of old age, compelled him to retire into private life about two years ago. His mental faculties becoming more and more impaired accounts in a great measure for the sad suicide.

1895

World Events

- Oscar Wilde writes *The Importance of Being Earnest*.
- Death of Lord Randolph Churchill.
- The Conservatives are back in power under Lord Salisbury.
- The National Trust is founded.
- Rontgen discovers X-Rays.
- Marconi invents wireless telegraphy.
- The first prom concerts are held in London.
- H.G. Wells writes *The Time Machine*.

A bazaar was held at St Mary's Parish Church in April 'for the purpose of improving Comber Church'.

> The Rev. Canon Smith ... roughly estimated it would take £300 or £400 to carry out the work; he had not the slightest doubt, when the ladies undertook the work, but it would be carried out successfully.

Eliza Pirrie, the grandmother of Thomas Andrews, died on 21st April. Thomas was left a legacy of £200 in her will. She also left a like sum of money to the Non-Subscribing Church in Comber 'for the purpose of keeping in good order and repair the meeting-house, schoolrooms, and church grounds'.

Her daughter, also Eliza (Thomas' mother), had a stained glass window in the church dedicated to her memory in 1923.

The Twelfth of July celebrations took place in a field at the end of The Crescent granted for the occasion by Mr James G. Allen. There were further celebrations at the end of the month with the defeat of Mr Gladstone's Liberal Party in the general election:

> ... a large bonfire, built on a hill of Mr Thomas Andrews, was lit by Mrs John Andrews, who before doing so, said she trusted that the bright flame of this bonfire, with those on the surrounding hills, and those also over loyal Ireland, might dispel the dark cloud of Home Rule which for years has hung like a pall over Ireland. Several speeches were made, her Majesty's name was duly honoured, and the names of the members of the Cabinet were received with loud cheers. The large assembly then separated, rejoicing at the result of the greatest general election of our time.

1896
World Events
- Cecil Rhodes resigns as Prime Minister of Cape Colony following his complicity in the Jameson Raid into the Transvaal. Kruger Telegram sent by Wilhelm II provokes crisis in Anglo-German relations.
- *Daily Mail* newspaper is launched.
- Repeal of the Red Flag Act, requiring vehicles to be preceded by a man carrying a red flag; speed limit raised from 4 to 20 miles per hour.
- Nobel Prizes are established.
- The first modern Olympic Games are held in Athens.
- Klondyke gold rush begins.

The new chancel at St Mary's Parish Church was consecrated on 4th January. Also dedicated at this time were two windows. The East Window was presented by Mrs Allen of Unicarval in memory of her late husband George who had died in 1886. George Allen was a farmer who had built up one of

Detail from Dorcas window dedicated at St Mary's in 1896

the best pedigree herds of Shorthorn cattle in the United Kingdom. He sold it at a massive auction in 1883. The window depicts Faith, Hope and Charity. And there was the Dorcas Window, in memory of Mary Watson Birch, who died in 1891. She was a sister of George Watson Birch, a former rector of St Mary's, and her father had also ministered there. Like Dorcas in the *Book of Acts*, she was known as a benefactress of the poor. The Birches were related to Thomas Ledlie Birch, minister of 1st Saintfield, who was involved in the 1798 Rebellion.

A young clerk aged 26 employed by the Distillery took his own life:

> It appears that he left Comber on Wednesday forenoon about eleven o'clock for his father's residence, who is a farmer at Lisbarnett, and arrived there about an hour later, where he remained till about five pm. He then left the house about that hour, taking with him a collie dog, and proceeded across a field adjoining the house. In a short time afterwards the dog was heard making a most fearful noise, howling and barking. The deceased's brother, who heard the noise of the dog, proceeded to the field, and on approaching where the intelligent animal was standing was horrified to find his brother lying on the ground in a pool of blood, with a gash in his throat which extended from ear to ear.

Comber point-to-point races, now an annual event, had to be switched to Groomsport, because farmers had broken up and cropped the course:

> Most people would have preferred having the meeting at Comber, which is so easy of access, and where every spot of vantage for a good view of the races is so well known.

North Down Cricket Club had seen phenomenal success since first winning the Senior Challenge Cup in 1887. They had chalked up further victories in 1888, 1890, 1891, 1892, 1893 and 1894. They did not win in 1896, but to make up for their disappointment they shared the Senior League title with Cliftonville in this, the inaugural year of the competition.

It was also decided to form a hockey club. At a meeting on 24th August Oscar Andrews was chosen as captain and W.T. Graham as secretary and treasurer. A hockey pitch was marked out at the Castle Lane side of the Green and first practice arranged for 26th September. Two early results were victories of 8–0 and 6–0 over Cliftonville and Ards respectively.

Comber Presbytery met on 7th September:

> Rev. Dr Taylor, availing himself of the liberty granted him by the General Assembly at its last meeting, resigned the active duties of the pastoral office in Second Comber.

This was shortly after the death of Dr Taylor's father. He had ministered in Comber for 18 years. Dr Taylor would continue in active service within the Presbyterian Church, doing valuable work as secretary of the Orphan Society and becoming Moderator of the General Assembly in 1899. Meanwhile Second Comber were looking for another minister.

1897

World Events

- Bram Stoker publishes *Dracula*.
- The Tate Gallery in London is opened.
- First taxis begin operating in London.
- Automobile Club of Great Britain is founded.
- Queen Victoria celebrates her Diamond Jubilee.
- Death of the composer Brahms.

The Rev. Robert James Semple, a licentiate of the Strabane Presbytery, was ordained in Second Comber on 5th January:

> The congregation was well represented on the occasion, and there was a very large contingent of friends, clerical and lay, some from long distances. The solemn services were commenced by the Rev. William Smyth, Killinchy, who preached an eloquent and practical sermon ... The Rev. Dr T.S. Graham ably expounded the principles of Presbyterian Church polity. The prescribed questions were put by the Moderator, Rev. Samuel English BA, and Mr Semple having renewed his subscription to the Westminster Confession of Faith, was ordained by prayer and the laying on of the hands of the Presbytery – the Moderator leading in the supplications. The newly-ordained minister having received the right hand of fellowship from the members of Presbytery and a large number of brethren from other Presbyteries who were present, the senior minister of the congregation, Rev. D.A. Taylor, delivered a most practical, pointed, and in every way admirable charge to his colleague and the congregation. In the afternoon, at three o'clock, the members of Presbytery and a large company of friends were entertained to dinner in the Manse by the congregation.

The point-to-point races were back in Comber again on 10th April:

> The day was beautifully fine, and as a consequence the attendance was large and representative. Lord Londonderry, as usual, officiated as starter, and after the races Lady Helen Stewart gracefully presented the prizes to the victors.

As usual, the races provided a good day's sport, but unfortunately Mr George Arthur's horse Starch had to be destroyed after a nasty fall at one of the fences.

Medallion struck to commemorate Victoria's diamond jubilee

There was also trouble resulting in James McBride of Glassmoss and James Harrison of Belfast being summonsed for a violent assault on James Arthur Aicken of Bangor. Harrison got two months' imprisonment with hard labour.

Tuesday 22nd June was the day of Queen Victoria's diamond jubilee:

> Comber excelled itself on Tuesday night. Never in the memory of the oldest inhabitant was the village so brilliantly illuminated. Some of the largest business establishments were almost covered with flags, Chinese lanterns, and other brilliant illuminations and decorations. Mr John Ritchie was supposed to carry off the palm, and Mr Andrew Smyth's establishment was a good second. The taste displayed by some of the humblest cottagers with flowers and candles in their windows deserves all praise. A huge bonfire blazed on Maxwell Court Hill, a second in the Square, and a third near the railway station. A torchlight procession paraded the town, accompanied by the Spinning Mill Brass Band and followed by a large crowd, which at intervals cheered for the Queen. The proceedings came to a close in the Square, where Mr Thomas Andrews made a short speech, referring to some of the principal events and discoveries during the Queen's reign, and complimenting the people on their loyalty and enthusiasm. The band played the National Anthem, cheers were again given for the Queen, and the crowd dispersed.

Unfortunately George Anderson, a barber who resided in Comber Square, was drowned in July while bathing in Strangford Lough:

He had gone with two companions to the lough to bathe, and it is believed that while in the water was attacked with a cramp, as he sank without any suspicion on the part of his companions that anything was wrong.

Comber was honoured with a royal visit on 6th September by the Duke and Duchess of York [the future King George V and Queen Mary]. There was a little ceremony when their train pulled into Comber Station on its way from Newtownards to Castlewellan:

> The guard of honour here ... was composed of members of the Royal Irish Constabulary. On the platform there were assembled the principal residents of the town and district, who, as the Royal train drew up, gave expression to their feelings of enthusiasm in orthodox fashion. As soon as the train had come to a standstill Miss Blizzard, daughter of Mr Blizzard of the Comber Distilleries, stepped forward to the door of the Royal saloon and presented to the Duchess of York a handsome bouquet, which her Royal highness graciously acknowledged ... An address of welcome was afterwards presented to the Prince and Princess by Mr John Andrews, senior magistrate of the town and district ... The Royal train was then shunted on to the main line, an operation which only occupied a few minutes' time, and as it departed from the station a local band played "God Bless the Prince of Wales".

The royal train paid a visit to Comber in 1897

There was a further stop at Comber on the way back:

> A pleasing little ceremony occurred here, when Miss Alice Patton, who
> was introduced to their Royal Highnesses by Mr Thos Andrews,
> presented to the Duchess, on behalf of the workers at the Comber
> Spinning Mill, a beautiful floral bouquet.

Once again North Down won cricket's Senior Challenge Cup, beating
North of Ireland in the final at Ormeau by 174 runs. They also completed a
double by holding on to their League title. They would repeat this double
success in 1898. The hockey team entered a newly formed League. Up until
November they had won every match they had played. But in that month
they were lucky to scrape a 2–2 draw with the North Staffordshire Regiment,
and this was followed by defeats against Antrim and Ards. Any chance of
winning the League had disappeared.

1898

World Events

- Kew Gardens in London are opened to the public.
- The Local Government Act for Ireland provides for the election of
   county and district councils.
- Britain recovers the Sudan following General Kitchener's victory at
   Omdurman.
- Pierre and Marie Curie discover radium.
- Count Von Zeppelin constructs an airship.

A meeting of tenant farmers was held at Comber on 22nd March for the
purpose of forming a local branch of the Ulster Tenants' Association, a body
working on non-sectarian and non-political lines, which had become firmly
established in the North of Ireland. Indignation was expressed against certain
landlords who were seeking to deprive their tenants of the benefit of the
Ulster Custom [option of renewal upon termination of a lease], and there was
a call for rent reductions and an end to dual ownership of land.

Davies' Paragon Circus was in town on 28 September, boasting their latest
novelty, the Princess Velise, the strongest lady on Earth. At every performance
she would lift ten of the heaviest men in the audience.

There were serious floods in October, the worst in fifteen years. Mr John W. Ritchie gave his opinion:

> With regard to the recent floodings ... I am not one of those who would point to the sewer as the cause, but would incline to blame the eccentricities of the rivers which flow past Comber, and occasionally overflow their banks ... The flooding at the Pound Bridge was caused by the water being thrown back from the dam in connection with the old flour mill, the sluices not being sufficient to meet the abnormal demands made upon them ...

The problem at Bridge Street was similar, caused by the weir or battery across the river which diverted water to the Lower Distillery dam. Mr Ritchie suggested putting in sluices across the battery, and that these could be lifted at times when the water levels got very high.

DAVIES' PARAGON CIRCUS,

AND UP-TO-DATE VARIETY,

NOVELTY AND GRAND SPECIALITY COMBINATION,

WILL Visit COMBER, WEDNESDAY, September 28; NEWTOWNARDS, THURSDAY, September 29; BANGOR, FRIDAY, September 30; DONAGHADEE, SATURDAY, October 1.

LEVIATHAN PERFORMANCES DAILY.

Afternoon—Open at 2 o'clock, commencing at 2-30. Evening—Open at 7 o'clock, commencing at 7-30.

Very Expensive and Costly Engagement of The Latest Novelty, THE PRINCESS VELISE, The Strongest Lady on Earth.

The Princess Elind at every performance will lift ten of the heaviest men in the audience. Absolutely the best and most diverting entertainment travelling in Ireland.

Prices of Admission, 3s, 2s, 1s, 6d. School Children 2d each at 2 o'clock.

The circus comes to town

1899

World Events

- The Boer War breaks out in South Africa.
- First motor bus runs in London.
- Edward Elgar composes *The Enigma Variations*.
- Launch of the White Star liner *Oceanic*.

The health of Comber's citizens was improving. According to Dr Henry's report:

> The number of deaths registered has never been so low in my time, and undoubtedly the effect of the new sewers in the town has been to

diminish sickness a very great deal, and not only that, but people are stronger and healthier, and no epidemic, and no person died from consumption or allied diseases, and I must say that now, since people are beginning to understand the reason and the imperative necessity for strict precautions as regards the destruction of the sputa, that cases of consumption are becoming much rarer.

Comber District Nursing Society was also making a significant contribution to the health of the district. Nurse Fitzsimmons had now settled in and Dr Henry thought that the decrease in mortality was largely due to her efforts. The ladies of the committee also came in for praise, especially Mrs T. J. Andrews and Mrs Herbert Andrews. The latter had made fortnightly visits with the nurse and supplied soup on Tuesdays and Fridays to those who had need of it.

Thomas Andrews of Ardara became a member of the newly formed Down County Council in March. However, in the same month the Comber solicitor William Shean died. He took an interest in sport, including North Down cricket and hockey clubs, and was a member of Second Comber Church.

Rev. Semple formed a company of the Boys' Brigade at Second Comber. They held their first display in May in front of a large crowd, when Mr Buchanan, president of the Belfast Battalion, was inspecting officer:

> The boys were drawn up under their officers, Captain James Smyth and Lieutenants Robert Smyth, Robert McDowell, and David

Rev. Semple and 2nd Comber Boys' Brigade

Caughey. Miss Toberson having favoured the audience with a pianoforte solo, the boys gave a very creditable display of company drill, and went through the physical exercises in a manner that reflected the greatest credit on themselves and their officers. Five young ladies now gave a musical selection, and at a later stage of the proceedings again favoured those present with another song. Indian club and dumbbell exercises were given by squads of the company, and another pianoforte solo by Miss Toberson. A "drill down" competition, for two gold and two silver medals, besides a book prize, was perhaps the most interesting, and certainly the most exciting, item on the programme.

In June summer was in the air and farmers were encouraged by the improved condition of the crops, which had been suffering badly on account of the recent heavy rain. One Comber gentleman was not so happy with the sunshine:

On Tuesday a man named Robert Beers, after coming home from hay work, fell opposite his own door. It was thought he was dead. Dr Henry was sent for, and on his arrival he found the unfortunate man was suffering from sunstroke.

In these days of climate change we would find that hard to imagine.

1900

World Events

- The sieges of Ladysmith and Mafeking are relieved in the Boer War.
- Coca-Cola goes on sale in Britain.
- The Labour Representation Committee (Labour Party) is founded.
- Boxer Rising in China against Europeans.
- The cake-walk is a new dance.
- Sibelius composes *Finlandia*.
- Cellophane is invented.
- The London Underground is electrified.

Britain was fighting a war in South Africa against the Boers, and in February a large crowd gathered to bid their farewells to three young men (James

Murray, Alexander Kerr and James Niblock) who had joined the Imperial
Yeomanry and were off to the fighting:

> On the arrival of the eight o'clock train at Comber, on which the
> recruits had come from Belfast, they were received at the station by a
> vast crowd, who sang patriotic songs. A procession was immediately
> formed and, headed by the Comber Flute Band, a start was made for
> the Orange Hall.

Thomas Andrews of Ardara chaired proceedings in the Orange Hall,
referring in a speech to the relief of Kimberley and the 'greatest general the
world could produce – Lord Roberts'. He added that 'the war was a justifiable
one, and no doubt the result would be a success for the British arms'.

Dr Robert Henry read a formal address, after which the young men were
each presented by Mrs Thomas Andrews with a pair of field glasses and a
knife, while Mrs Thomas James Andrews presented each with a box of
cigarettes and a sleeping helmet.

At long last North Down had success on the hockey field. And they won
not just one competition but two. Firstly in February they defeated Antrim

Comber Flute Band

3–2 in the final of a new competition – the Keightly Cup – played at the Green in Comber. This was the only year when this was played for on a knock-out basis, in future years being presented to the winners of the Senior League. The second trophy won by North Down was the Kirk Cup in April when they defeated Cliftonville 4–2 in the final.

The capture of Pretoria from the Boers in South Africa was celebrated in June in some style:

> ... a great number of houses honoured the occasion with flags and bunting. In the evening when the workers had quit work every preparation was made in the way of making bonfires ... The Gillespie Cycling Club added greatly to the amusement of the evening by turning out in fancy costumes. There were 36 dressed in all the latest fashions; they paraded the streets, causing great amusement to all. The Comber Flute Band was also in attendance, together with Mr James Dugan, who preceded the procession on horseback, carrying a Union Jack in hand. At about 9-30 the bonfires were set ablaze, the cycling club riding round and adding effect by the display of their fancy dress. At this time Kruger [Paul Kruger, the Boer leader] appeared, carried by a few willing hands towards the fire. He was made examine his last resting place before being cremated ...

The Comber Will Case made big news. This related to the will of the late James Withers who had died in December 1899. He had destroyed his first will shortly before he died. By the revised will he left £600 to be invested in Government stock, and bequeathed the interest on that, together with the rent of three houses, to go towards increasing the salary of the minister of Second Comber Presbyterian Church, at that time Rev. Robert Semple. The will was contested by Mary Logan of Trooperslane, Carrickfergus, who alleged that the deceased had not been of sound mind at the time the will was made and that he had been unduly influenced by others, including Rev. Semple. The jury found in favour of the three plaintiffs in the action, who claimed to be executors of the will – Rev. Semple, William James McCartan and Mary McMillan.

Election fever was in the air in the autumn, with North Down being contested by Colonel Sharman-Crawford and Mr T.L. Corbett, a Scotsman standing for the working classes against the landlord interest. Mr Corbett addressed a large meeting in Comber Orange Hall where he outlined his aims, which included better housing for the workers and a scheme for old-age pensions. In October he held a monster meeting in the Square, to which he was accompanied by Comber Flute Band and a large crowd from the railway lines on the Newtownards Road, about half a mile out of the town. Comber was undoubtedly a stronghold for Mr Corbett, and when the poll results were announced later that month there were great rejoicings at the news of his victory. Mr Corbett again visited the town on the afternoon of the announcement, thanking the local agent Mr F. J. Orr and all his supporters for the splendid victory. In the evening tar barrels were lit in the Square, and fires could be seen on all the prominent hills in the district. Another celebration in November took the form of a conversazione and meeting in a field lent for the occasion by James Cairns of Cherryvalley. Two large marquees were erected, one for teas, the other for the meeting. This had seating for 2,000 people and standing room for as many more. Each speaker was wildly applauded, and at intervals throughout the evening thunderous cheers were raised for Mr and Mrs Corbett.

Comber was being kept in the dark:

> It would take one gifted with the sure-footedness of a mule to walk through Comber on a dark night, especially on the north side of Mill Street. What's wrong with the Gas Company? They evidently don't want to light up on moonlight nights, when the atmosphere is covered with dense black clouds, so thick that no moon can be seen. Surely there is something wrong. The Gas Company are expected to throw some light on the matter.

A new pub called The Paragon was opened in High Street by Mr John W. Ritchie:

John W. Ritchie letterhead

Mr Ritchie pushed open a beautiful glass door and I entered ... finally my eye caught the department where the liquor was kept. The bottles were beautiful and clean, and all arranged out in an order that was most pleasing to the eye, having for their background well-finished mirrors ... The counter is of American style, well studded with shining panels. The ceiling is nicely squared off, while the floor is beautifully laid out in tessellated tiles, resembling large blue stars. For the convenience of those who want to be private, neat little compartments are at hand, composed of pitchpine, with mahogany mouldings, and ornamented with various crystalised glass. There is also a fireplace in it of the most quaint description. At each side are two figures cleverly carved out of Scrabo stone, looking rich and antique. In fact, the "Paragon" is a first-class bar, neat, up-to-date, and comfortable, while the prices are the same as anywhere else.

1901

World events

- Death of Queen Victoria; Edward VII succeeds.
- Assassination of US President William McKinley; succeeded by Theodore Roosevelt.
- Commonwealth of Australia comes into being.
- Marconi transmits messages across Atlantic by wireless telegraphy.
- First petrol-engined motor bicycle in Britain.
- Boxer Rising in China suppressed.
- Walt Disney born.

Not only a New Year, but a new century has dawned. How did the good people of Comber see it in? This is what the 'Comber Eagle' wrote in the *Newtownards Chronicle*:

> ... I had several good laughs on Monday night last at some Comber people who were watching for the New Year. They have some amusing superstitions, indeed. As soon as twelve o'clock struck, one man in Mill Street rushed to the front door and threw it open to the wall, just to let the New Year in. A party in High Street sat round in a circle in dead silence until the last stroke of twelve, when they all jumped up, as if they suddenly sat down on the business end of a pin, and wished one another a Happy New Year. A woman in Bridge Street swept out the kitchen and hall a few minutes to twelve o'clock, for she wanted no old year dirt in her house ... Perhaps the best of all was a well-known Comber man, who got hit on the back of the neck about Killinchy Street, with a small paper bag of flour, while a number of voices shouted, "A Happy New Year", and made off. A novel salute indeed.

But the new century brought a touch of sadness with it. The Victorian era came to an end with the death of the 81 year old queen on 22nd January. Comber went into mourning:

> On the 27th January appropriate sermons were preached in the different churches in Comber. Nearly all were suitably and tastefully draped for the solemn occasion, and the discourses listened to with becoming reverence. In Second Comber Presbyterian Church the Rev. R.J. Semple MA ... referred most feelingly to the many virtues and

graces of the late Queen, and bore many tributes to her many sterling qualities of head and heart.

And on the day of the funeral a memorial service was held in St Mary's Parish Church.

> The service consisted of part of the burial service, with additions. An address was given by the Rev. Canon Smith to an unusually large congregation. The Dead March in "Saul" was most effectively played, after which the congregation slowly dispersed.

War against the Boers was in full swing out in South Africa, and some of Comber's young men were given a rousing send-off:

> The members of the Comber Reading Club met in the Orange Hall to bid farewell to some members who are leaving for the front to join Baden-Powell's Constabulary. Tea was served at 7-30, and after this had been disposed of, a smoking concert was held, at which Dr Henry (president of the Reading Club) presided ... The troopers for the front were afterwards given a hearty reception. On Saturday night a large crowd assembled to see them off at the station, where they were heartily cheered. A great many of the townspeople travelled to Belfast, and saw the recruits off at the Liverpool boat.

Smoking concerts seem an unusual form of entertainment, but at the time they were very popular, and in September another one would be organised, this time by North Down Cricket Club.

This was Census year, and all heads in Comber were counted on the night of 31st March – the grand total of 2,095 souls.

The census for Belfast showed Thomas Andrews, aged 28, living at 11 Wellington Place. He had the rather important sounding job of Assistant Shipyard Manager.

A new shop opened in Bridge Street:

> Mr Edward Collins of Comber, whose new grocery establishment in that town was opened during the year, is to be congratulated upon the taste and enterprise displayed in the general arrangement. The premises are fitted in the most up-to-date manner, and the stock fresh and well-assorted, which shows that Mr Collins knows his business, and bids fair to make his shop an attraction to the public. He has also introduced the incandescent light, which is a great improvement.

Mickey White

In addition to the grocery, Mr Collins has fitted up a splendid laundry in the town, where all the latest machinery is to be seen working, and we understand patrons are delighted with the completeness and finish of the washings entrusted. An important factor, too, is that prices are 20 per cent cheaper than city laundries. With a few men of the enterprise of Mr Collins, Comber would rapidly become a place of great business activity.

In May the Comber football team travelled to play local rivals Ards FC. It ended in fisticuffs. Ards were 3–0 up within fifteen minutes, by which time:

the play was now getting a trifle rough, and the visitor's left back, Allen, on charging little Harvey very heavily, the latter retaliated with the fists. Some of Comber players now left the field.

They were persuaded to return, however, and the match resumed without major incident until, with the score now at 4–1 to Ards,

Atcheson, at close quarters, was about to head the ball through, when Harrison, the visitor's custodian, intentionally struck him in the face with both hands, knocking him down. The spectators now rushed for Harrison, who decamped at top speed, and it was with difficulty he was guarded to the pavilion, the game ending in an unsatisfactory way.

Spare a thought for the poor old ref, none other than Mickey White of Comber, who 'should have exercised his authority in putting down any attempts at rough play, no matter who the offender was'.

Also in May, we had the Fancy Dress Cycle Parade, a popular form of entertainment at the time. It took place at the North Down Cricket ground, and was run by Second Comber Presbyterian Church in aid of funds for renovating the church buildings. The Cricket Club themselves needed funds, and in August held two events. The Saturday event was an athletic sports meeting, which, unfortunately, was a washout:

North Down Cricket Ground, Comber   Co. Down

Carnival day at the cricket grounds

In consequence of the sodden condition of the track, grass-spills were frequent in the cycling events, but nothing of a serious nature occurred. The five miles cycle race was run in a downpour of rain, which the spectators could not withstand, and the final heat was witnessed by a very small number of enthusiasts.

The Cycling Gymkhana of Wednesday afternoon was more successful:

The costumes were in their way triumphs, and the scheme of decoration pursued by some of the aspirants for honour in the comic competition displayed much originality, and created a great deal of merriment. In that in which the gentlemen appeared there was a really excellent assortment of quaint characters, tramps, stage Irishmen, the old woman that lived in the shoe, and reproductions of a couple of Pears's well-known pictorial advertisements, the naughty boy, actually carried by a competitor, with a basin and an assortment of soapsuds in front ... while in the other items Britannia, so to speak, jostled against Spanish maidens, flower girls, and milkmaids, making figuratively a mosaic that appealed with much effect to the representative gathering of spectators. A very acceptable feature of the programme was the musical ride, in which four gentlemen and four ladies took part. The leader was Mr Burton Smith, and the figures gone through were, with certain necessary variations, a replica of the cavalry musical ride to be seen at military tournaments.

OUR LOCAL EXPRESS
Belfast to Comber
and back in one day

The Comber train fails to disturb a tranquil game of cricket

No surprise that North Down were in the final of cricket's Senior Challenge Cup. After all, they had already won it nine times since its inception in 1887. But what a fiasco! The Northern Cricket Union had arranged the match against North of Ireland for the day of North Down's athletic sports and would not change it. The cup was awarded to North of Ireland.

It seems that the trains were not up to speed, and the Belfast and County Down Railway found themselves the butt of a number of jokes. At a concert in Comber, Ards Minstrel Troupe asked where the BCDR were first mentioned in the Bible. The answer was apparently in Genesis – 'When the Lord created all creeping things'.

And the weather, as usual, provided a major talking point. This report occurred in November:

> I never experienced such weather as visited this district on Tuesday. The blustery weather, accompanied as it was by the largest downpour of rain within my memory, wrought much devastation. Between Comber and Dundonald large areas of the country were completely inundated with water, and in some places the floods were so deep that the occupants of a number of houses were compelled to seek refuge in the upper apartments of their dwellings. The railway line was submerged, and the trains had to proceed with considerable caution. I trust it will be a long time before such a visitation comes our way again, as considerable loss has been sustained all over the country.

1902

World Events

- Boer War in South Africa ends with Treaty of Vereeniging.
- Arthur Conan Doyle writes *The Hound of the Baskervilles*.
- Aswan Dam in Egypt completed.
- 20 dead and 200 injured when terracing collapses at football match between Scotland and England at Ibrox, Glasgow.
- Mont Pelée volcano in Martinique erupts and destroys the town of St Pierre; 38,000 are killed.

Comber farmers have for many a year ploughed their furrows in the fields around the town. What could be more natural than to hold a ploughing match?

> Under the auspices of the Comber District Ploughing Society, an inaugural competition took place on Tuesday on the farm of Mrs Shaw, Cattogs, Comber, and proved an unqualified success. The society, of which Mr Thomas Andrews, Ardara, is president ... has only recently been formed, the meeting of Tuesday being its initial effort so far as regards ploughing competitions. The interest in the match was shown by the large number of entries, as well as by the crowds of spectators who were attracted to witness the contest from the immediate and surrounding districts. The land on which the ploughing match took place was admirably adapted for such a competition, while the fair weather which obtained throughout the day obviated any postponement of the contest ... The skill displayed by those engaged in the match was of a very high order, and ploughs of both Irish and English makes were well to the fore in the competitions.

Table tennis (or ping pong to give it its good old-fashioned name) was the craze of the day:

> On Friday evening a very successful ping pong tournament took place in the schoolhouse in connection with First Presbyterian Church. There was a good attendance, and the entries in the various competitions reached a large number. Master Willie Andrews proved himself the best of a good lot entered for the gentlemen's singles competition, Miss Edith McRoberts won the honours in the ladies'

Mrs John Andrews,
née Sarah Drennan 1807–1902

competition, and Miss M. and Mr Sam McKee played splendidly together in the mixed doubles competition. There were two tables kept going, and great interest was manifested in the various heats.

The death took place of Mrs John Andrews, the former Sarah Drennan, at the advanced age of 95. She was the widow of John Andrews who had built Comber Spinning Mill, which he never saw in operation, having died a few weeks before its opening in 1864. She was also a grandmother of Thomas Andrews Junior:

Mrs Andrews ... was a daughter of the famous Dr William Drennan of Cabin Hill, Belfast, a man who as physician, author and politician played a conspicuous and honourable part in the public life of Ulster in the latter part of the eighteenth century and the beginning of the nineteenth.

This Dr Drennan was one of the men credited with founding the United Irishmen in 1791. He was also a noted poet who first applied the name of 'Emerald Isle' to Ireland.

Mrs Andrews leaves three sons, of whom the eldest is the Right Hon. William Drennan Andrews PC, LLD, one of the judges of his Majesty's High Court of Justice in Ireland; the others being Mr John Andrews JP of Comber and Mr Thomas Andrews of Ardara. She also leaves a daughter Frances, wife of Mr Edmund W. Garrett, barrister-at-law, of Epsom, a Metropolitan police magistrate, and numerous grandchildren.

Comber Fair took place in April:

The half-yearly hiring fair was held on Monday, and the attendance from the surrounding country of servants to be hired for the term beginning in May, and of farmers to employ them, was as usual large, as this is the principal hiring fair in the northern part of the county. Wages ranged from £3 to £6 for the half-year for girls and women, with board; and for boys and men from £6 to £9, also with board. This is not an advance on previous wages, but in odd cases more was given. There were a few cattle in the fair, but nothing exceptionally good or for which a high price was given ...

Unfortunately, drunkenness and fighting were common occurrences on these occasions, and Comber's constabulary were kept on their toes.

Success for North Down Hockey team, winners of the Kirk Cup for the second time in their short history. The final against Cliftonville took place at Sydenham before a large crowd of spectators:

The ground was in grand condition, and the sun shone brightly all the afternoon, so that the match was thoroughly enjoyed by everyone present.

Kirk Cup Winners – 1901/02
Back row (left to right): Walker, S. Davidson, T.J. Macdonald, J. Niblock
Middle Row (left to right): N. De Wind, R.F. Kerr, H.D. Todd, J. Ritchie, J. Macdonald
Front row (left to right): Russell, D. Smyth

At full time the score was 1–1.

> It was agreed to play an extra ten minutes each way, but after the time
> had elapsed the score was still one all. Further extra time was then
> agreed on, although both sides by this time had palpably had enough
> of it. This settled the result, for shortly after the bully-off Macdonald
> scored for North Down. Although Cliftonville made a plucky effort,
> they were repulsed, and when the last "extra" was up North Down
> were left winners of one of the hardest tussles the Cup competition has
> ever produced or is likely to produce. Score – North Down 2 goals,
> Cliftonville 1 goal.

Comber White Flag LOL 244 had a new banner unfurled at the Orange
Hall before setting off for the field at Ballynahinch on the 12th July:

> ... The banner is a beautiful piece of work – white silk – and was
> supplied by Mr William Bridgett, Belfast. The picture on one side is
> that of King William, and on the other side "The Secret of England's
> Greatness". This banner was much admired all day, as also were the
> members. The number of members in the lodge was the largest of any
> lodge in the field, and all wore new white silk sashes, making a
> splendid sight ...

The conscientious folk of Comber, along with their neighbours in
Newtownards, wanted to get to their work in good time. An early train was
needed:

> The workman's petition for an early morning train to leave
> Newtownards early enough to arrive in Belfast before six o'clock is
> being extensively signed ... Leaving Newtownards a little after five
> o'clock and calling at Comber for passengers, the train would arrive in
> Belfast in time to allow workmen to pursue their various occupations,
> and would enable them to return in the evening to their respective
> homes and enjoy the healthy country air.

The petition was successful, as evidenced by the following reply from the
Belfast and County Down Railway Company:

> I am instructed to inform you that the train will be put on as from 1st
> November, provided at least forty men sign their names guaranteeing
> to travel from Newtownards each week-day, and likewise ten from
> Comber.

The Coronation of Edward VII eventually took place on 9th August, having been postponed from June due to the king's illness. Comber celebrated:

> The town was decorated, and presented a gay appearance; the handsome statue to the great General Gillespie in the centre of the Square was artistically clad in flags, laurels etc. The children of the town and neighbourhood were invited to a field near Ardara by Mrs Thomas Andrews, where games were indulged in and prizes liberally provided. In the evening the houses were illuminated, and a bonfire was burned in the Square, after which the Comber Flute Band, whose much appreciated services are always available, led the way to the high hill overlooking the railway station and town, where another huge bonfire soon lit up the entire neighbourhood. Hearty cheers were given for the King and Queen with the greatest enthusiasm ...

John Miller Andrews, eldest son of Thomas Andrews of Ardara, was married on 10th September at Rivington Unitarian Church, near Bolton in Lancashire. His bride was Jessie Ormrod. The best man was the groom's brother, Thomas Andrews Junior, who was making a successful career in shipbuilding. After their honeymoon the young couple were enthusiastically welcomed back to Comber:

John Miller Andrews with his bride Jessie Ormrod

They were met at the railway station by all the members of the family of Mr Thomas Andrews. The approach of the train was announced by the explosion of a quantity of detonators. All the houses along the route from the station to Ardara were profusely decorated with flags and bunting. After sunset the good folk of Comber combined to give them a welcome by sending up rockets and lighting a large bonfire, which had been made ready convenient to Ardara, and which burned for over three hours, and must have been seen for miles around. The Comber Flute Band enlivened the proceedings by playing numerous airs during the evening. Mr John M. Andrews and his father, Mr Thomas Andrews, made short but tasteful speeches, thanking those who had so honoured them.

James Milling died in November:

Mr Milling was one of the leading merchants in Comber, and was possessed of more than average business capacity. His death will be keenly felt in the district with which he was so long associated, and we sympathise deeply with the family in the severe loss they have sustained. The funeral took place on Wednesday, and the evidence of the late Mr Milling's popularity was shown by the very large cortege which followed the remains to their last resting-place.

James Milling – the family business
dated back to 1731

1903

World Events

- King Alexander I of Serbia and Queen Draga are assassinated.
- Emmeline Pankhurst forms the Suffragette Movement.
- Wright Brothers make first successful flight in an aeroplane with a petrol engine.
- First motor taxis in London.
- First Teddy Bears made in USA.

John Andrews JP died in March:

> It is with feelings of the deepest regret that we have to announce the death of this well-known and highly esteemed gentleman, which took place on Saturday evening at his residence, Comber. The deceased ... was a member of the firm of John Andrews & Co., flax spinners, Comber, and was a brother of the Right Hon. Mr Justice Andrews and Mr Thos Andrews, Ardara, Comber. He took an active interest in public affairs, and for many years served as a member of the County Down Grand Jury and of the Newtownards Board of Guardians until ill-health prevented him undertaking duties of this kind. In politics he was a Liberal Unionist, and in several of the Parliamentary elections in County Down he played a prominent part ... Mr Andrews leaves a widow and family of two sons and two daughters to mourn his loss ...

The state of the roads around Comber was coming in for criticism:

> The roads from Belfast to Newtownards and to Comber have been condemned at a meeting of the Roads Improvement Association, held last week. A resolution was passed, in which it was stated these roads were a disgrace to a prosperous locality, and further, that no road metal should be laid down unless where a proper and systematic use of the steam roller was in operation.

And there were problems with the mail which were raised in Parliament:

> In the House of Commons on Wednesday Mr T.L. Corbett MP asked the Postmaster-General whether, seeing that the train which leaves Newtownards with the English mail 6-25 pm passes through Comber

at 6-35 pm, he could arrange to carry the mail from Comber by it, instead of the letters being sent by bicycle or on foot, as at present.

The matter was successfully resolved.

Mr Corbett was also in action as the main speaker at the Twelfth demonstration, held in Comber:

> On Monday forenoon a great demonstration of the Orangemen of the Ards district was held at Comber under fairly satisfactory weather conditions. From an early hour the brethren were astir, and the sound of drum and fife was heard everywhere. Judging by the proportions of the meeting it is quite evident that the men of the Ards are still as true to the traditions of their Institution as ever. Considerable interest was manifested in the proceedings owing to the presence of Mr T.L. Corbett MP, the popular member for the constituency, who drove over from Newtownards shortly before one o'clock, in company with the Rev. Wm Wright. The honourable gentleman on his arrival on the field was greeted with loud cheers. It is safe to say there were many thousands of people present. The meeting was held on the Crescent Hill, on the road to Newtownards, which was kindly lent for the occasion by Mr John Allen.

Thomas Andrews of Ardara was in the news:

> The honour of being appointed a member of his Majesty's Privy Council in Ireland has been conferred upon Mr Thomas Andrews of Ardara, Comber, one of the best known and most highly-esteemed residents in the County of Down.

And a new Roman Catholic priest was appointed:

> His Lordship the Most Rev. Dr Henry, Bishop of Down and Connor, has been pleased to appoint Rev. G. Crolly, St Patrick's, Belfast, to be Parish Priest of Newtownards and Comber ...

Comber was not immune from disease, and in December:

> Dr R. Henry reported there was an outbreak of diphtheria in Comber. He recommended that the National and Sabbath schools be closed for three weeks, and that posters be put up through the town urging on the people the necessity for keeping their yards clean, and also the desirability of boiling all water or milk before using.

1904

World Events

- War breaks out between Russia and Japan over rival interests in China.
- Russian fleet causes outrage in Britain when it fires on British trawlers in the North Sea.
- *Entente Cordiale* between Britain and France settles differences over Egypt.
- The independence of Tibet is established.
- Construction of Panama Canal begins.
- Company of Rolls-Royce is formed.
- Puccini's opera *Madame Butterfly* is first performed.
- The *Daily Mirror* newspaper is founded.
- J.M. Barrie writes *Peter Pan*.
- First electric main-line train in British Isles runs from Liverpool to Southport.

There was some controversy at the annual Comber Point-to-Point Races held in April. An objection was raised against the winner of the Farmers' Race, a horse with the nowadays politically unacceptable name of 'Nigger':

'An objection was lodged to the winner on the grounds that it was a horse called Le Marquis, and had competed in other races'. This was against the rules. The objection was upheld.

Mr James G. Allen of Comber brought a new industry to the north side of Comber Square:

> This industry is the manufacture of patent oil road rollers, and to Mr James G. Allen, who is the sole leasee of the French patents for Ireland, are we indebted for its introduction, especially as they will be manufactured in his own works at Comber. The advantages claimed by oil road rollers over the present steam-driven rollers are that they are better for road-making, simplify the work, and economise fuel, labour, time, and upkeep, so much so that it will reduce the cost of road-making very much. ... on Monday last, when it had its first trial round Comber Square, every part worked as smoothly as if it had been at work for months.

Ransomes, Sims, & Jefferies, Ltd., Traction Engine

Sold by JAMES NIBLOCK, Mill Owner, COMBER.

Advertising postcard

Another industry in the town was of course the manufacture of the famous Old Comber Whiskey (in production since 1761). A former partner in the business died:

> The death of Mr J. McCance Blizard, Comber, on Wednesday will be heard of with much regret by everyone who had the pleasure of knowing him. Mr Blizard was for years the managing director of Comber Distilleries (Limited), and in that capacity discharged his duties to the satisfaction of his co-directors and the public.

The Roman Catholic School opened on 10th October. While later in the same month the town got a new dance hall – the Thompson Hall:

> A long-felt want has been supplied by Mr John Thompson, who had built a new hall in Mill Street for public gatherings and recreations ... The hall was opened on Tuesday night with a social gathering when about 180 mustered. Mr W. Farquhar acted as chairman for the evening. He said that he thought it was a privilege to wish success to the local enterprise of Mr Thompson, who was well known and very highly respected in Comber. ... There was a well-varied programme, including the well-known "cake-walk", which can be danced to perfection in Cummer.

Crowds outside the Thompson Hall. Note the railway arch in the background

A child was found abandoned at the Upper Distillery premises:

On Wednesday Sergeant Finnegan, in charge of Comber police force, was apprised of the fact that a female child had been found on the Comber Distillery premises in Killinchy Street. It appears that as James McCullough, carter in the distillery, was in discharge of his duties at a quarter past six o'clock in the morning he discovered a bundle in the yard connected with the stables. On examining the bundle he discovered it to be a female child, aged a few months, in exceedingly poor condition. The child was poorly clad, but had been supplied with a feeding bottle fairly well filled. The police were communicated with, and Dr R. Henry's assistance was secured. The ambulance of the Newtownards Union was sent for, and the child was conveyed to the workhouse, where it at present remains. There is as yet no clue as to how the child was placed in the stable yard, but the police are making diligent inquiries and hope soon to be able to arrest the guilty party.

1905
World Events

- Revolution in Russia sees workers killed in St Petersburg on Bloody Sunday and mutiny on the warship *Potemkin*. Tsar Nicholas II agrees to an elected Parliament.
- Japan annihilates the Russian fleet and captures Port Arthur. The war ends with the Treaty of Portsmouth.
- Kaiser Wilhelm II visits Tangier and sets off the first Moroccan crisis.
- Norway becomes independent of Sweden.
- Sinn Féin is formed in Dublin.
- Automobile Association is founded in London.
- Albert Einstein publishes the *Theory of Relativity*.
- Neon signs are first displayed.
- Franz Lehar writes the opera *The Merry Widow*.
- Aspirin goes on sale in Britain.

Thomas Andrews has worked his way up to become Chief of Design at Harland and Wolff at the early age of 32.

Tragedy struck in High Street with the death of a little girl:

> It appears that on the 16th January the child's clothes caught fire while she was in the house, and, in spite of efforts made to extinguish the flames, the poor creature suffered painful burns on various parts of her body. The parents at the time were absent at work, but there was an elder girl in charge of the house. Dr Henry was in attendance, and did his utmost for the suffering child, but she died early on Wednesday morning.

Unfortunately this type of incident was all too common in those days.

Sergeant Edward Finnegan had been in charge of the Comber police since 1895. He now decided that it was time to call it a day:

> Sergeant Finnegan in his every dealing has proved himself a most efficient officer, at the same time always showing much discretion in the discharge of his onerous, and at times difficult, duties. Formerly, he was stationed in Newtownards, where he also gained the esteem and confidence of the townspeople by his urbane manner and the

creditable way in which he performed his obligations to the public, and the body to which he had the privilege to belong. We trust that there are many days of happiness in store for Sergeant Finnegan, whose popularity as an officer of the force could not well be surpassed.

A branch of the North Down Unionist Association was formed in Comber, the venue Comber Orange Hall:

> The following delegates were elected – Chairman of the District, The Right Hon. Thomas Andrews; secretary, Dr Henry; treasurer, Mr Matthew Kerr. The other delegates elected were – Messrs John W. Ritchie, Comber; John Whitla, Ballyaltikilligan; David Hamilton, Ringcreevy; Hugh Skillen, Comber; and John Gourley, Ballyrussell.

A Grand Masonic Bazaar was held for three days in the grounds of the Non-Subscribing Church, under the auspices of Masonic Lodge Temple of Fame No 46, Comber:

> The brethren of Temple of Fame Lodge having some time ago come to this conclusion that it was an absolute necessity for them ... to have a house and habitation of their own, set their minds to work ... A block of property in Castle Street, which had formerly been in the possession of the late Mr John McConnell JP, having been put on the market, No 46 promptly purchased it for £400, fee simple. ... To thoroughly equip and complete the hall and to render it suitable for use, an expenditure of something between £200 and £300 will be necessary, and the bazaar, which was inaugurated under such happy auspices on Thursday, had been organised in order to raise the necessary funds to meet the debt incurred ... Thursday was an ideal day, and ... large marquees were erected on the grounds in order to provide accommodation for the many beautiful articles of work which were displayed on the various stalls ... In the evening the scene was enhanced by excellent lighting arrangements ... At the hour appointed for the opening ceremony – 3 o'clock – a very large number of people had assembled in the grounds, and punctual to time the Marchioness of Londonderry arrived in her motor car ... In the adjoining lecture hall the Freemasons were assembled, and ... seldom have we seen such an imposing procession as it wended its way from the hall to the marquee where the opening ceremony was to take place ... The attractions of the bazaar included concerts, competitions of various kinds, and a host of amusements, Mr McCormick's XL orchestral band supplying excellent music.

Interior of Comber Methodist Church, demolished 1995

On 11th August a social meeting was held in the Methodist Church, Comber, on the occasion of Rev. Charles Clayton's move to Enniskillen:

> The church was beautifully and artistically decorated for the occasion by several friends, and presented a charming appearance ... Mr Lockhart and Mr Thompson ... presented to Mr Clayton, on behalf of the members and friends of Comber Methodism, a very handsome illuminated address and "Special Rudge-Whitworth Cycle" with lamp and all complete.

Coursing was a popular sport, and the North Down Coursing Club was formed:

> A meeting to start the above club was held in the Brownlow Arms, Comber, on Tuesday 19th September, and a good number of the leading coursing men in the district attended. It was decided to hold a meeting on the Barnhill meadows, kindly lent by Mr S. Stone JP, on the 17th October.

Scarlet fever arrived in the town:

> The Clerk [of Newtownards Rural District Council] reported that there was an epidemic of scarlet fever in the Comber district, and

apparently people were not aware of the danger of mixing with patients and those in attendance. He recommended that posters should be put up throughout the district, requesting people not to mingle in any way with the patients or the attendants on patients, until certified free from infection, and that the Council in future enforce the Prevention of the Notification Act, which required the head of a family on becoming aware of the disease and the medical practitioner in attendance, to forthwith report the matter to the medical officer of health.

1906

World Events

- Henry Campbell-Bannerman wins a Liberal landslide election victory.
- A French appeal court declares the innocence of Alfred Dreyfus, wrongly convicted of treason 12 years earlier.
- Germany plans to build a fleet of battleships. Britain launches *HMS Dreadnought*.
- Transvaal and Orange Free State win self-government from Britain.
- John Galsworthy begins *The Forsyte Saga*.
- 700 people die when an earthquake rocks San Francisco.
- First rugby international between England and France.
- Belfast City Hall opened.

Election fever was in the air, and Mr Corbett retained his seat for North Down:

There was great rejoicing on Monday night over Mr T.L. Corbett's victory for North Down, and bonfires were to be seen on nearly all the high hills. The Comber Flute Band paraded the town, and a large crowd followed to Robb's Hill, where there was a big bonfire lighted, and stirring speeches were delivered ... The following night one of the largest crowds ever seen in Comber assembled in the Square. The local flute band, with the Ballygowan Flute Band, marched out, accompanied by a big crowd, to meet Mr and Mrs Corbett, who were coming from Newtownards. The horses were taken out of the brake, and it was pulled right up to the Square, where a large bonfire was blazing, and Mr and Mrs Corbett were received with tremendous cheering.

John Patton sustained a bad injury at the Comber Races:

> He had the mount on King Hal, who after falling in the dip, was again remounted by Mr Patton. On coming down the hill for home, however, King Hal again blundered, and horse and rider came a heavy cropper. As both horse and rider lay for some time on the ground, the spectators thought that both or either of them were killed. This fortunately did not turn out to be the case, as after Mr Patton was pulled to the one side of the course out of danger from the other horses following, King Hal got on his legs again. Dr James Moore, examining Mr Patton, found that he had sustained a severely fractured collarbone.

Comber's wedding of the year took place at the Non-Subscribing Presbyterian Church when Eliza Montgomery Andrews (known as Nina), daughter of Thomas Andrews of Ardara, was married to an Englishman, Lawrence Arthur Hind:

> There was a very large and fashionable congregation, most of the leading families in the Counties of Down and Antrim being represented ... There was no house without its flag or its string of streamers, while the factory was transformed out of all recognition by the lavish use of bunting and coloured drapery ... The railway station was also bright with flags ... Across the roof of the church festoons of evergreens, relieved by sweet-scented roses and other flowers, were suspended, and along each of the aisles there had been erected three floral arches, under which the bridal party passed ... Crowds of mill workers, who had been given a half-holiday ... collected in front of the church and showered handfuls of rice and confetti indiscriminately on the guests as they arrived.

> Shortly before half-past one the bride walked into the church, leaning on the arm of her father, and followed by her maids ... The bride looked exceedingly pretty in a dress of white satin, trimmed with Brussels lace ... She also wore a wreath of orange blossoms and white tulle veil ... She carried a bouquet composed of white orchids, lily of the valley, and white Lady Bountiful carnations.

Well-wishers outside the church

The marriage ceremony was performed by the Rev. Thomas Dunkerley, minister of the church. A quintet provided choral music, under the direction of Herr Louis Werner, who presided at the organ.

The church festooned with greenery

Inside the marquee at Ardara where the reception was held

... amongst those present in the church were the Marquis and Marchioness of Londonderry, Mr Justice Andrews, Right Hon. J.W. Pirrie and Mrs Pirrie, Sir Otto and Lady Jaffé, Sir J.B. and Lady Dougherty, Mr G.W. Wolff MP, and Mr and the Hon. Mrs Kennedy.

Reception menu card

After the ceremony the newly-weds left the church to the strains of Mendelssohn's Wedding March. Outside they were

greeted with showers of confetti, and as they drove to Ardara, where a reception was subsequently held, ringing cheers were raised ... The guests were entertained in a large marquee, one hundred feet long, with polished floor, the property of the Ulster Menu Company, who had entire charge of the catering.

A programme was provided by the band of the Inniskilling Fusiliers. Afterwards Mr and Mrs Hind set off on their honeymoon to the South of Ireland.

Group photo from the wedding album, taken at Ardara

Unfortunately, this marriage was to have an unhappy ending. Colonel Hind was one of the victims of the Battle of the Somme in 1916, and his name is engraved on Comber War Memorial among the list of the fallen. Nina died in 1930, aged only 56 years old.

* * * *

The new Masonic Hall in Castle Street was dedicated:

> The exterior of the building presents a fine, substantial appearance, with its newly done-up, stone-finished frontage. Over the door, "Masonic Hall 1906" is deeply cut, and on the fanlight, on a five-pointed star, is the No 46. The floor of the hallway is neatly laid out with Mosaic work, a finely-wrought six-pointed star facing the entrance ... The mystic lodge room has been done up and furnished in an elaborate yet tasteful manner ... The W.M.'s chair sits in a beautifully formed archway, and over it is suspended the mystic letter "G", hanging from the keystone of the arch, on which is appropriately inscribed "Silentia, virtute et amore". ... On the walls hang many examples of knowledge of the Craft, produced by Br John Robinson, The Flow, Comber, who is recognised as an authority on all matters Masonic.

All was not well at the hockey club:

> At a meeting of the Council of the Ulster Branch of the Irish Hockey Union held in Belfast on the 11th May a report was made as to the

behaviour of two members of North Down Club at recent matches directly under the jurisdiction of the Ulster Branch. The matter having been thoroughly discussed, it was unanimously decided that this sort of conduct could not be permitted to continue, and that (1) these two men be suspended for life from all participation in Ulster Hockey; (2) that no club should under any circumstances utilise their services either as players or as referees; (3) that any club playing with them or against them or acting under them as referees shall also be suspended.

Much better news for North Down's cricketers who brought a successful season to a conclusion when they won the Senior League for the first time since 1898.

Success also for the Spinning Mill Airgun Club:

The secretary's report showed that the "A" team were champions of the Newtownards and District Air-Gun League, and also that the "B" team occupied a respectable position on the League table of last season.

A serious fire occurred in Bridge Street at the premises of Edward Collins:

Sergeant Flannigan and Constable Lockhart were immediately on the scene, and by this time a goodly number of the inhabitants of the town were soon in the vicinity. As Comber has no fire apparatus of any kind, the above gentlemen and the police immediately organised a willing band of workers. Water was carried in buckets from all the pumps in the vicinity, and after three hours' hard work their efforts were crowned with success, having confined the fire to its source. If it had caught Mr Collins' shop and dwelling-house, which at one time was feared, nothing would have saved that side of the street.

The *Newtownards Chronicle* was pleased to announce a reduction in the price of gas:

Our readers in Comber will be pleased to learn that after November 1st the price of gas will be reduced by 10d per thousand cubic feet. This reduction in price should encourage non-consumers of gas to use it for lighting purposes more generally, as against the use of inflammable oils, which at all times are risky and dangerous. It will not be out of place to mention that the Comber Gas Light Company supply the public lamps in Comber with free gas, which is rather unique in the public lighting of towns.

Former gasworks office

A sensation was caused when a body was found on the site of Comber Racecourse:

> On Sunday morning the police at Comber were informed by Mr
> David McDonald of Castle Hill that he had found the dead body of a
> man lying in the stream near the old castle grounds in the vicinity of
> the racecourse. Constable Walsh went at once to view the body with
> several civilians. The body was found lying on the back in a deep
> "shough" about nine feet in depth, and amongst the very long grass of
> over three feet in growth, and behind a big whin bush, so that it was
> difficult to see. Constable Walsh obtained a large canvas sheet, and
> with the aid of Messrs Hugh Skillen, Samuel McGreegan, John Allen,
> Robert Patton, James Dugan and Joseph McIlveen wrapped the body
> in it, then placed the remains on a door and carrying them to the old
> mill. The face and skull were completely without flesh, also the hands
> and part of the chest, the rats having left the lower part of the body
> untouched. It is surmised that the body may have lain from last
> Comber steeplechases. There was nothing in the pockets to lead to
> identification ...

The body was later identified as that of a pensioner named Thomas
Watson, who had resided in Brownlow Street, Comber, until about ten weeks
ago, when he left his residence, and had not been heard of since. He was a
former soldier, a hero of the Afghan War.

The Cooneyites were a popular religious group at the time. A police report reads:

> Remained most of the time about The Square where a Cooneyite meeting was being held about 9pm. The Cooneyites left the Square and went along Mill Street. They were followed by a rather disorderly crowd.

The Council were debating the lighting of Comber:

> Mr Kerr ... said it was absolutely necessary that Comber should be lighted, as in some parts of the town a stranger coming along in the dark was apt to stumble, and be hurt ... Dr Henry said he had a memorial signed by 300 of the people of Comber, and he might say that the proposition had the support of practically every person in Comber. He had a letter from Mr J.M. Andrews, in which he stated that he and his father were anxious to see the town properly lighted, while Mr Bruce of the Distillery and the Rev. Mr Semple were also in sympathy with it. The only light they had at night in some parts was the moon, and sometimes it forgot to come out ... The motion to appoint the committee with a view to facilitating the lighting of the town was passed unanimously.

1907

World Events

- Kingston, Jamaica is destroyed in an earthquake, and 1,000 people killed.
- Robert Baden-Powell founds the Boy Scouts.
- New Zealand becomes a Dominion.
- The Irish State Jewels are stolen from Dublin Castle.
- Music Hall stars go on strike over pay.
- 2 people are shot dead as a dock strike cripples Belfast.

Thomas Andrews is now Managing Director of Harland and Wolff.

The Island Hill Regatta had been a local attraction for some years now. But there was some doubt about its future:

A meeting of the members constituting this now well-known Strangford Lough club was held ... on Tuesday evening. Mr J.G. Allen (commodore of the club) presided ... It was agreed that part of the funds should be expended on marking off, by buoys, likely dangerous spots in the northern portion of the Lough. Arrangements having been made for the ensuing season, the question of the annual regatta was discussed, but its fuller consideration was left over until a later date.

Tragedy visited Comber in the guise of a couple of drowning accidents. The first involved a boy named McFadden who fell into a dam and was drowned. The other was a respected farmer called Alex Baxter of Ballyaltikilligan:

On reaching the spot which is known as the "Long Hole", Mr Baxter decided to bathe, Mr Kennedy advising him to be careful, as in case of accident he would be unable to render assistance. Scarcely had Mr Baxter entered the water than he threw up his arms and sank. Mr Kennedy waded in to assist him, but without success. He then went to Messrs Murray's of Cherryvalley, which is in close proximity. A small punt was procured, and with the aid of this the body, which was lying in about nine feet of water, was recovered by Mr John Murray.

Further tragedy occurred at Cattogs, outside the town:

On Saturday evening last, about four o'clock, a little girl named Mary Quinn, aged five years, daughter of Isaac Quinn, Cattogs, was accidentally burned to death. It appears that Mrs Quinn had occasion to leave the house, and on returning met the little one running out with its clothes all on fire. So serious were the burns that Dr Henry was called upon. Despite all that medical skill could do, the child died the same night.

The Good Templars were a body devoted to temperance and enlightening people to the evils of alcoholic drink. A lodge was formed in Comber:

Although Comber compares favourably with other places in this respect, it has been felt for some time that there was need for more thorough and aggressive temperance work ... The meeting on Tuesday night was further evidence of this missionary spirit ...

The International Order of Good Templars – membership certificate

The Rev. Mr Dunkerley ... said it was a matter of fact that intemperance filled our jails, lunatic asylums, and workhouses, which institutions had to be supported by men like himself who would not allow strong drink to cross their lips ... After the meeting a lodge was instituted ... and forty-five new members enrolled.

Mr Allen had an unexpected encounter with a bread cart:

On Tuesday an accident, which might have resulted in more serious consequences, occurred near Comber. A two-horsed bread van of Messrs McWatters was being driven into the town, and met on the road a new oil motor roller of Messrs J.G. Allen & Co., Comber. A collision occurred, the exact particulars of which cannot yet be gleamed, but the result was that the driver of the bread van was thrown off his seat and got his leg broken in two places. He was subsequently removed to Belfast Hospital. One of the horses was slightly injured, but nothing to any serious extent.

McWatters bread cart

The Northern Bank lost one of its stalwarts:

The sudden death of Mr Samuel Farquhar, cashier in the Comber branch of the Northern Bank, which occurred early on Wednesday morning at his residence, Bridge Street, Comber, caused somewhat of a sensation in the town with which he has been so long identified. His genial presence will be much missed not alone in Comber, but also in many of the surrounding towns, where he was always a welcome guest at social meetings ... Mr Farquhar was a ... zealous member of Second Comber Presbyterian Church, and was nearing sixty years of age ...

North Down Cricket Club were celebrating fifty years of their existence:

A grand bazaar was thought to be the most fitting way of celebrating ... The practical idea of placing the club in a sound financial position was the main one in connection with the promotion of the present bazaar ... A sum of between £300 and £400 will be required for the erection of the proposed new pavilion, which, it is hoped, the bazaar will easily wipe off ... The finely-appointed grounds surrounding the Unitarian Church were kindly placed at the disposal of the club for the bazaar, and a more ideal or charming situation could not have been selected ... Most of the stalls were erected in a huge marquee placed in a central position in the grounds, and there was a large assemblage in the latter tent when the opening ceremony took place at a temporarily-erected platform.

Countess Annesley declared the bazaar open, after the usual speeches.

In connection with the bazaar and carnival the "Go-as-you-please" competition [an early form of marathon], the last two miles of which will be run on the grounds of the North Down Cricket Club, will not be the most uninteresting feature. The competitors will leave the Variety Market, Chichester Street, Belfast, punctually at 1-15 o'clock, and will proceed to Comber Cricket Grounds, via Newtownards. The competitors may be expected in Newtownards shortly after two o'clock.

The excitement was mounting in Comber Square where 'the various runners were loudly cheered, Lee being especially accorded an ovation, and Mr McKinley, the Ballycastle veteran, the oldest competitor, and young Shannon of Belfast, a mere lad, getting great encouragement from the people'. Lee of Ulsterville Harriers was the eventual winner, ahead of his fellow club member Weatherall and Kennedy McArthur from the South African Constabulary, but originally from Dervock, County Antrim. The latter had the distinction of going on to win the gold medal for the marathon at the 1912 Stockholm Olympic Games.

Mr Chambers with the pupils of 1st Comber National School

First Comber School lost its headmaster, after the resignation of Mr Chambers, principal since 1886:

> On Friday evening last, November 29th, Mr James Chambers, principal teacher of First Comber National School, was presented with a purse of sovereigns subscribed by members of the church and a few other friends on the occasion of his resigning owing to ill-health. Mr Alexander Caughey, who made the presentation, referred in feeling terms to Mr Chambers' long connection with the school and popularity in the district. The Rev. Dr Graham, manager of the school, and Mr Wm Magowan, Troopersfield, also spoke of Mr Chambers in eulogistic terms.

The new principal was Mr James Millen, previously head teacher at Portaferry.

1908

World Events

- King Carlos and Crown Prince Luis of Portugal are assassinated.
- Herbert Asquith becomes British Prime Minister.
- William Taft is elected US President.
- Bulgaria is recognised as an independent country.
- Kenneth Grahame publishes *The Wind in the Willows*.
- 150,000 are killed in an earthquake in Sicily.
- The cricketer W.G. Grace retires.
- Jack Johnston becomes the first black world boxing champion.
- Olympic Games are held in London.
- Emmeline and Christabel Pankhurst, leaders of the Suffragettes, are sent to prison for inciting a riot.

The Council were discussing the state of Comber Square:

> Mr Kerr drew the attention of the Board to the fact that the clay was showing up on the roadway of the Square at Comber. He had spoken to the surveyor about the matter, and the latter said he had not sufficient road metal. He thought the Board should give directions to have the matter attended to.

Meanwhile sacrilege had been committed with the mass burglary of several of Comber's churches, all in one evening:

> When early on Saturday morning the sexton of Second Comber Presbyterian Church, which is in charge of Rev. R.J. Semple MA, opened the building, he was astonished to find the interior in a state of disorder. A closer inspection convinced the sexton that a burglarious entry had been made, and this view was confirmed on discovering that one of the windows had been forced open, while it was also evident that the locks of several presses in the vestry had been tampered with. The police were at once communicated with, and while the constables were making a minute inspection of the premises, word was received that the Parish Church, the Methodist Chapel and the Roman Catholic Church had also been broken into. Subsequent investigation led to the conclusion that the same party was concerned in all four of the burglaries, as the methods adopted were similar, the objective in each instance being apparently the procuring of money.

Thomas James Andrews 1847–1908

The death occurred of Mr Thomas James Andrews, who lived in the Big House in the Square:

He was a most prominent man amongst the public, and was well liked by all who had the pleasure of knowing him. He was always interested in public matters, but his heart leaned towards the promotion of good sport, which he always encouraged. He was one of the gentlemen who initiated the popular Point-to-Point Races at Comber, and was ... also a promoter of the present North Down Cricket Club, and it is in the lands of Mr Andrews that the cricket grounds are situated ... Deceased was ... the son of the late Mr Isaac Andrews, of the well-known firm of Messrs Isaac Andrews & Son Ltd, Belfast; brother of Mr John Andrews, the present owner of the Belfast Mills.

There was also a wedding in the Andrews family involving the son of Thomas James' cousin, Thomas Andrews of Ardara. The groom was Thomas Andrews Junior himself, his bride being Helen Barbour of Dunmurry. The ceremony took place in Lambeg Parish Church on 24th June. The couple went to live at Dunallen in Windsor Avenue, Belfast.

There was a serious accident on the railway at the Glassmoss crossing, out the Newtownards Road:

Thomas Anderson, the gatekeeper, being caught by the engine which runs down to Newtownards to bring the workmen's train to the city. Dr Robert Henry of Comber was quickly in attendance, and found Anderson suffering from a badly fractured skull, and his face cut down as far as his nose. Everything possible was done for the poor fellow, and later in the morning Dr Henry again visited him, and found that he had rallied a little. He was then conveyed by special train to Belfast, then per ambulance to the Royal Victoria Hospital. Strange to say, he is progressing well.

Another death occurred in a house fire:

A pensioner of the Royal Irish Constabulary named Cantwell met with his death at his residence in Comber on Thursday under shocking circumstances. The bed in which he was lying caught fire, and he was terribly burned about the legs and lower part of the body before his cries brought assistance ... It is supposed that the fire was caused by the smouldering of a piece of cloth which was wrapped round a hot water bottle ...

Second Comber got five new elders:

> Messrs John T. McMillan, William Henderson, James Moore, Samuel B. Drake and Joseph Berkeley were ordained with prayer and the laying-on of the hands of the Presbytery ...

The pupils of Smyth's School at Second Comber put on a grand exhibition:

> On Friday evening last a more than usually interesting entertainment, consisting of a concert and display of physical drill, was given by the pupils of the above school. This was the first concert of its kind in Comber, and the greatest interest was taken in it, so much so that at the hour of opening the large schoolroom, capable of seating about four hundred people, was filled in every part ... This school has always taken a very high place in the educational interests of the community. The inspectors' reports have always been of the very highest, but during the past year its success has been almost phenomenal. The school has grown so rapidly that addition had to be made to the teaching staff, and still we understand that growth goes on ...

Indeed all Comber's schools got top marks when it came to sanitation:

> There were good water-closets in First and Second Comber, also the Mill School, and the others had earth closets, which only required keeping clean to be right ...

The Twelfth again took place in Comber:

> A large and enthusiastic demonstration under the auspices of Comber District No. 15 was held on Monday in a large field situated a short distance from the town, the use of which was kindly granted for the occasion by the Messrs Milling. The local brethren, who were joined by a number of district lodges, assembled outside the railway station, and, headed by their respective bands, playing patriotic and appropriate tunes, marched in processional order to the field ... The weather unfortunately was of the worst possible description. Rain fell

in torrents during the early part of the day, but this fact did not lessen the enthusiasm of the brethren ...

The main speaker was Captain James Craig MP, who fulminated against the spectre of Home Rule.

North Down's cricketers won the Senior Cup against Cliftonville, an achievement long overdue. The final at Ormeau:

> was marked by the brilliancy of play by the Comber team ... They ran up a score of 250, the principal contributors being Joe MacDonald (45) and W. Coulter (45) (not out). When Cliftonville went to the wickets the veteran Tommy Graham and Crawford played such havoc with the stumps that the whole team was put out for the small score of 76. Following on on Monday Cliftonville did much better, and knocked up 204, leaving North Down to make 31 to win. This they did ... It was a great victory for the Comber men ... Although always in the fighting line for the senior cup, it is nine years since they won this trophy. May it find a resting-place in Comber for many years to come.

The hockey team were also once more among the honours, sharing the Kirk Cup with Malone.

In the wake of the Old Age Pensions Act, a committee met regularly to determine those who were entitled to a pension in Comber:

> A meeting of the Comber sub-committee was held in the Newsroom of the Comber Spinning Mill on Monday 16th November at four o'clock ... The Clerk submitted fifty-five claims, of which forty-seven were allowed, two adjourned, and six disallowed.

1909

World Events

- Old Age Pensions are payable in Britain to those aged over 70.
- House of Lords rejects the Budget.
- Henry Ford manufactures the Model T car.
- Louis Bleriot flies across the English Channel in an aeroplane.
- Harry Ferguson makes the first Irish flight.
- Robert Peary reaches the North Pole.
- First motion picture newsreels shown.
- First colour films screened in Britain.

A train crashed through the level crossing gates outside Comber:

> On Tuesday night, shortly after the 11-5 PM train from Belfast passed Comber on its way to Newtownards, the curiosity of the passengers was awakened by a crackling sound, and the train being pulled up. The cause turned out to be that the train had passed through the crossing gates, which had not been opened up when the train was due. After an interval the train proceeded on its journey, arriving in Newtownards some twenty minutes behind scheduled time.

Lord Londonderry was a popular man with his Comber tenants:

> A memorial having been forwarded to Lord Londonderry during his present visit to Mountstewart by the townpark tenants of Comber ... asking for a reduction in rents owing to the prolonged agricultural depression, his Lordship ... intimated his willingness to grant an all-round 15 per cent reduction, being desirous that the most friendly relations subsisting between him and his Irish tenantry should be maintained.

The County Down Rifle Club held its inaugural meeting in the Mill School:

Charles Vane-Tempest-Stewart,
6th Marquis of Londonderry 1852–1915

At the present time everyone was talking of the defences of the country, the navy and the army, and especially the navy ... They could not in Comber build Dreadnoughts. Unfortunately Strangford Lough was not deep enough to float them. But if they could not build Dreadnoughts they could do something to assist the other arm of the service, the army. The establishment of those rifle clubs would enable them in case of emergency to turn out a very considerable number of really good marksmen ... Lord Londonderry stated that he himself would be pleased to subscribe a challenge cup to be shot for annually ... the Craig family had generously presented them with a range at Castle Espie on Strangford Lough ...

A total of 55 members were initially enrolled.

The newly-opened cricket pavilion on a postcard of 1909

North Down Cricket Club got their new pavilion:

The pavilion attached to the North Down Cricket Club's ground at Comber has been enlarged at a cost of £300, and the opening ceremony was performed on Saturday afternoon by Mrs T.J. Andrews, whose late husband proved himself such a warm and devoted friend of the organisation. The pavilion is, to all intents and purposes, an entirely new building, for comparatively little of the old structure has been left standing, and, besides being an ornament to the ground, it should prove of inestimable benefit to the club and visiting teams on match days ... Mrs Andrews unlocked the door with a silver key which was presented to her for the purpose by the committee, and in the course of a happy little speech she said the North Down Club had a glorious record, and she was sure that the present members would do all in their power to maintain the reputation which it had built up for fair play, good play, and splendid hospitality ...

Comber's police sergeant was transferred:

Many friends in the Comber district will learn with regret of the departure of Sergeant Thomas Flanagan from the little distillery town. During his few years' residence the sergeant, through his fairness and general courtesy, made many friends, and much regret is expressed at his leaving. The best of wishes go with him to Banbridge. Sergeant Patrick Dinsmore from Annalong is the succeeding officer.

Housing was a major issue at the time:

Dr Henry O'Neill JP addressed a large meeting in the Square, Comber, in support of the movement for providing better housing accommodation for the labouring classes throughout the County Down. On arrival at the outskirts of the town, Dr O'Neill was met by the local band, accompanied by a large crowd, and escorted through the streets to the Square where, under the shadow of the Gillespie Monument, he addressed an enthusiastic meeting, the audience giving him a very attentive and sympathetic hearing. He explained to them the object of that and all similar meetings which was to organise the farmers and labourers of the district, so as to promote their welfare, to promote the brotherhood of labour, to secure for them the benefits conferred upon them by the Labourers' Acts, payment of 8s a week during sickness, the general improvement of the welfare of the worker, and the promotion of such legislation as will assist them and their families to live under more healthy conditions ... Many labourers' cottages had been built in Comber of a good type, but many more were required, and he urged upon the residents of Comber to press upon the Rural District Council the urgent necessity there was for having erected at the earliest possible moment a sufficient number of cottages to supply the reasonable demands of the labourers and artisans of the town and district ...

Comber was also the venue for a demonstration organised by the International Order of Good Templars. It was held:

... in a field kindly lent for the occasion by Mr Munn, The Cattogs, Comber. The meeting was arranged for by the Executive of the Newtownards District Lodge, in conjunction with the members of the Rising Star Lodge, Comber, and the undertaking was in every way a decided success. In addition to the Good Templar Order being largely represented from Ballygowan, Belfast, Comber, Donaghadee, Glastry, Greyabbey, Kircubbin, Newtownards, and elsewhere, quite a number of Rechabites and Sons of Temperance were also in attendance. There were crowds of sympathising friends too, who helped to swell the numbers considerably, so that altogether several thousand people were present during the proceedings.

A reduction in the number of licences for the sale of alcohol was called for, including those granted to spirit grocers, along with total Sunday closure of public houses and a ban on the use of alcohol in wine used for Holy Communion. The same venue would be used for a similar meeting in 1910. The Methodist Church showed 'a display of living pictures' in the Orange Hall:

... Fully an hour before the time announced for opening a crowd had gathered around the closed doors, and at eight o'clock every available seat was filled, in spite of the fact that extra forms were borrowed for the evening. The windows and every possible spot was utilised for seating purposes, yet many of the spectators who continued to pour in were compelled to stand ... A peep into the realms of nature was without doubt one of the most interesting, artistic and beautiful films of the display ... "The would-be acrobats" was a complete change. Laugh succeeded laugh at the mischievous pranks of two small boys. "How Percy won the beauty show" was also funny beyond description. Wright's aeroplane was a film that excited much interest ...

Comber Presbytery noted an interesting development:

... it is worthy of notice, as promotive of temperance and tranquillity, that the public-house on the brow of the hill in Comber, between the Square and the spinning mill, and close to the First Presbyterian Church and to the main entrance of the Unitarian Church, has been closed by the purchase of it on the retirement of its recent holder by representatives of the mill and the Churches mentioned, the proprietors of the mill generously subscribing £75 and members of the First Presbyterian congregation from £5 to 10s each, to the amount of £50, and members of the Unitarian congregation a proportionate sum to meet a deficit in the price-money of the house by its conversion to another use.

Edwardian Mill Street

This was what one Comber ratepayer thought of the town's streets:

> ... They are a disgrace to our civilised state. I am sure the like of them are not to be found in Europe. Every few yards the dirt is heaped up, and lying that way for months. When heavy rain comes, of course it washes it into the grates and chokes them, and the consequence is some of the houses are flooded. Persons crossing the street in the dark walk into these mud heaps almost up to the knees. It is not only unpleasant, but not conducive to the health of the town. The doors and windows in the houses of the inhabitants are in a constant state of dirt; motor cars and other vehicles send the mud flying in all directions ...

1910

World Events

- George V succeeds Edward VII as King of Britain.
- Two general elections in Britain.
- Union of South Africa becomes a Dominion.
- First Labour exchanges opened in Britain.
- Dr Crippen is hanged for the murder of his wife – transatlantic radio used in his capture.
- Florence Nightingale dies.
- Girl Guides founded.

William Drennan Andrews, elder brother of Thomas of Ardara, was one of the most respected High Court judges of his day. He had also unsuccessfully contested the County Down election of 1878. He decided to retire:

> As a judge he has always been held in high esteem, and the soundness of his decisions has seldom been disputed. He has had a long and varied experience of well nigh every kind of judicial work, and his opinions are highly valued by his colleagues on the Bench.

Later in the year the inhabitants of Comber organised a banquet in honour of Judge Andrews. This was held in the Non-Subscribing Church Lecture Hall.

Tragedy occurred at the Lower Distillery dam:

> About nine o'clock on Tuesday morning some of the workmen employed at Comber Distillery made a shocking discovery in the Lower Distillery dam at the bottom of Bridge Street, Comber, when they found the body of an elderly man. The deceased, who had apparently met his death by drowning, was identified as James Caughers, a man belonging to Newtownards. It is presumed that deceased fell into the dam whilst going along the street in the darkness of the previous night.

An inquest drew 'the attention of the District Council to the dangerous position of the place, where deceased probably walked into the dam'.

The Point-to-Point Races, normally held over a course at Mount Alexander, had a change of venue:

The annual point-to-point meeting organised by the North Down Harriers Hunt Club was held on Saturday at Carnesure, adjacent to Comber. Glorious weather favoured the fixture, and as a result a record crowd assembled on the hill to watch the events. A change was made in the course this year, and while it has the advantage of being over old grass, still the course is not all that is desirable from a spectator's point of view... The meeting was patronised by the elite of the Counties of Down and Antrim and the City of Belfast. The Marquis and Marchioness of Londonderry and house party were present, as was also the Lord Mayor of Belfast (Mr R. McMordie MA). The Master of the North Down Harriers, Mr J. Blakiston-Houston DL, entertained most hospitably a large number of guests to a sumptuous luncheon, and subsequently tea, in a special marquee erected on the grounds ...

Another innovation was the participation of a female jockey in the first race:

The distance was about three miles, and additional interest was evinced in the contest on account of the fact that a young lady was to ride in male attire. She weighed out in regular jockey's garb, and certainly looked as capable and fit to steer a winner as anyone in the tent. Miss Violet Cowen... is an accomplished horsewoman.

Traction engines may have been a great invention, but they were making an utter mess of the roads:

Mr Morrow drew attention to the state of the road between Comber and Dundonald. The County Surveyor explained that this road had been in excellent condition, but had been damaged by traction traffic during the winter. Dr Steele said that the traction engines were actually seen destroying a footpath, a fact which could be proved.

King Edward VII died in May, and the following resolution was adopted by the citizens of Comber:

That we, the inhabitants of the town and district of Comber, desire to express our sincere sorrow at the death of his Most Gracious Majesty King Edward VII, who during his reign conferred such inestimable services not only on his Empire but on the world at large. Their Majesties our present King and Queen, and the Queen-Mother and other members of the Royal family, have our profound sympathy in the loss of one so dear to them, and we trust that they may find some comfort in the knowledge that their sorrow is so universally shared.

The day of the funeral was observed as one of mourning:

Factories and business houses were closed, work of all descriptions was suspended, and householders marked the occasion by drawing their blinds from noon until five o'clock pm. A united memorial service was held in the Second Presbyterian Church, in which the following clergy took part: – Rev. Mr Dunkerley (Unitarian), Revs Dr Graham and Mr Semple (Presbyterian), and Rev. Mr Trotter (Methodist). There was a very large and representative congregation, amongst which was the Second Comber Company of the Boys' Brigade.

Comber District Nursing Society did important work in the town, and in the past year Nurse Findlay had made a total of 2,232 visits to 137 cases:

That the number of cases and visits is smaller than last year is owing to the fact that, except for an outbreak of measles and whooping-cough among the children, there has not been so much illness in the village, and the nurse is not allowed to visit houses where there is any infectious disease.

Gas lamp opposite the Brownlow Arms. Note the greyhound above the door

The Committee appointed to oversee the public lighting of Comber had been busy, and were now advertising for a lamplighter:

> Mr J.M. Andrews moved, and it was resolved – That the Committee recommend the Council to appoint Mr W.J. Stevenson as lamplighter at £15 a year as salary, which the Committee understand he is agreeable to accept. It was further resolved – That the Committee recommend the Clerk of the Council to prepare an agreement, to be signed by the lamplighter, embodying the conditions already fixed. He is to commence lighting in the evening at 4.40, and to commence extinguishing at daybreak; and at night to commence to extinguish at 10.15, except on Saturday night, to commence to extinguish at 11.15. It was also resolved – That the Railway Company be asked if they would be good enough to keep the lamp at the bridge lit for as long a time as the other lamps in the town.

Another League championship win was chalked up by North Down Cricket Club:

> The Comber Club can again congratulate themselves on having had a most successful season, as they won the Senior League competition, and out of 27 matches played 10 were won, 5 lost, and 12 drawn. They scored 4,049 runs for 169 wickets (average 23.96), as compared with 3,760 runs scored by their opponents for 225 wickets (average 16.71).

First Comber got seven new elders:

> This Presbytery met in Comber on the afternoon of the 17th October for the ordination of six elders and the installation of a seventh in the First Presbyterian Church of Comber. The Rev. William Smyth presided as moderator pro tempore. After a sermon by the Rev. D.H. Maconachie and an exposition of the office of ruling elder by Dr Graham, Messrs David Brown, Ballymaleddy; Hugh Chambers, Cherryvalley; Hugh McDowell, Ballalloly; William McKee, Drumhirk; William J. McMaster, Ballyloughan; and George Spence, Comber were ordained, and Mr Jas McCulloch JP, Granshaw, was installed in First Comber, the Moderator for the day leading in the prayer and act of ordination and installation, and the Rev. James Bingham following with a charge to the elders and congregation ...

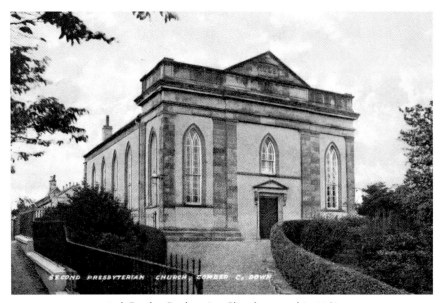

2nd Comber Presbyterian Church, opened in 1840

Meanwhile at Second Comber, the Rev. Semple had resigned, after accepting an appointment as professor at Magee College, Londonderry. At a meeting of Presbytery:

> It was stated that the Rev. Dr Vance officiated in Second Comber on Sabbath 23rd October, and declared the pastoral office vacant, and that the Commission in charge of the congregation consists of Rev. Dr Taylor, convenor, Revs Dr Graham, J. Bingham, and D.H. Maconachie, and Messrs James Berkley, Robert Dunn JP and John McCullough ...

Another man leaving Comber was Thomas Rankin:

> On Thursday evening the 17th November Mr Thomas Rankin was made the recipient of a very valuable dining-room clock and gold scarf pin in the schoolroom of the Comber Spinning Mills, from his numerous friends in the firm of Messrs John Andrews & Co. Ltd on the occasion of his leaving Comber to take up new duties in Belfast. The Right Hon. Thomas Andrews DL presided and made the presentation. In the course of his remarks he said that Mr Rankin had been with them for the past ten years as their foreman mechanic, and during all these years he had charge of the engines, boilers, dynamo, and all other machinery; and he (Mr Andrews) had no hesitation in

saying that Mr Rankin had discharged the duties devolving upon him with great ability and success, and to the entire satisfaction of all concerned.

It was a time of comings and goings, and Comber got a new bank manager:

"Mr James Park Cinnamond JP, who has just taken over the managership of the Comber branch of the Northern Bank, has a banking experience extending over thirty years. He began his career at the head offices of the Northern Bank, but for the last quarter of a century has been in the Cushendall branch, latterly as manager.

Thomas Andrews' daughter, Elizabeth Law Barbour Andrews was born on 27th November.

Thomas Andrews Junior with wife Helen and young daughter Elba

1911

World Events

- The power of the House of Lords is curbed and the period between elections is limited to five years.
- Lloyd George introduces the National Insurance Bill.
- Commons vote to pay MPs £400 per annum.
- An international crisis is created by the arrival of a German gunboat at Agadir in Morocco.
- Strikes by South Wales miners, London dockers and British railwaymen.
- A republic is proclaimed in China.
- Roald Amundsen reaches the South Pole.
- A gang of anarchists are besieged in a house at Sidney Street in London.

The new minister at Second Comber was Rev. Thomas McConnell, installed on 3rd May. He was described as the General Assembly's only ordained evangelist:

> There was a large congregation, the spacious church being filled... The solemn services were commenced by the Rev. Thomas McCaughan, Killyleagh, who after conducting the usual opening exercises of public worship, preached an able and instructive sermon... The prescribed questions were put to Mr McConnell by the Moderator of the Presbytery, Rev. W.K. McLernon BA, which, having been satisfactorily answered by him, he was set apart to his work by prayer ...

At a reception held on Thursday 4th May in the schoolroom adjoining the church, the ladies of the congregation presented Rev. McConnell with a pulpit gown and cassock.

The *Titanic*, the largest ship in the world, was launched in Belfast on 31st May. Thomas Andrews had played a major part in its design.

Souvenirs were in the shops for the coronation of King George V, including this one:

> Messrs Gordon, The Square, Comber, are giving away delightful souvenirs of the coming Coronation to all buyers of their "Coronation" blend of tea, at 2s per pound. The souvenir is in the

shape of a beautifully finished and decorated "Coronation" tea canister, or "caddie", and is embellished with very fine photo reproductions of their Gracious Majesties the King and Queen.

Commemorative postcard

And the children of First Comber National School received a special Coronation treat:

> When the usual routine of schoolwork was over, the pupils, numbering close on 200, assembled in the large room and were supplied with tea and cake very kindly provided by Mrs McBurney [of Moatville, Ballyrickard], who was assisted in dispensing it by the teachers and a number of lady friends. After tea, each boy and girl was presented with a Paragon China cup and saucer of very pretty design, the gift of Mr Hugh McBurney. Dr and Mrs Graham, Mrs Millen and teachers each received a Coronation souvenir from Mr McBurney. Mr McBurney's great desire seems to be to make others happy, and with his usual thoughtfulness he brought his fine gramophone and delighted all present with selections.

Mr James G. Allen of oil roller renown had meanwhile struck it rich:

> Three years ago... he left for Cuba and, with the experience he acquired some years ago in gold-seeking in South Africa, he started at

once prospecting for gold. His many friends in the County Down will be glad to learn that in this he was most successful. After securing the mining rights of some 700 acres of land, he discovered five good gold-bearing mines on this grant, which he sold to an American company shortly before he left Cuba at a very large sum ...

Circus visits Comber 1911

A new banner was unfurled by the Comber True Blues Orange Lodge:

On Saturday evening ... there was a band and drum parade through the principal streets of the town. The procession was joined in by the band of the Boys' Brigade, the old band of the town and a number of drummers from the various local lodges. Having assembled at the Orange Hall, where there was a large crowd, Miss Stone of Barn Hill gracefully unfurled the splendid new banner, the bands playing the National Anthem... After the conclusion of the interesting proceedings the bands paraded the town, each marching to its own headquarters – Second Comber schoolroom and the Spinning Mill schoolroom respectively.

Canon George Smith, rector of St Mary's since 1868, was forced to retire due to ill health. His successor was Charles Manning, the rector of Muckamore. A few weeks later Canon Smith was dead:

As a clergyman, he attended most faithfully to his duties, and was ever foremost in any movement for the welfare and elevation of the people. Wherever he went, his presence was cordially welcomed, and his counsel and advice so tactfully given was always eagerly sought. By his parishioners he was held in the warmest affection. His decision to resign aroused among them the profoundest sorrow, and as an indication of their feelings towards him they resolved to supplement the pension to which he was entitled from the Clergy Superannuation Fund, and to allow him to reside in the Rectory during his lifetime ... He was regarded as a man of shrewd judgement and sound common sense, and his remarks, which were always practical and to the point, received great attention ... In politics he was a staunch Unionist, but he never took any active part in politics, and he was connected with the Orange Institution.

A Unionist Club was organised in Comber:

Rev. Charles Campbell Manning,
rector of St Mary's

A largely-attended and enthusiastic meeting was held on Tuesday evening in the Orange Hall, under the presidency of the Right Hon. Thomas Andrews, when the preliminary steps were taken for the formation of a Unionist Club for the town and district ... The Chairman outlined a scheme for the holding of a monster demonstration of Ulster Unionists in London in order to express their determination not to submit to Home Rule ...

Alexander Byers of Railway Street, a boy of 5 years old, was drowned:

The lad was returning from First Comber Presbyterian Church School to his home when his coat got into the water, and in reaching to recover same the little lad overbalanced himself and fell into the stream that runs past the Spinning Mill. Mr William Andrews soon heard of the accident, and about twenty minutes afterwards recovered the body, which had been carried down by the flooded stream into the dam below the mill. Sergeant Dinsmore and Constable Singleton were quickly on the scene, and every effort was made at resuscitation. Dr Steele soon afterwards arrived, and he pronounced that life was extinct.

1912

World Events

- War in the Balkans between Turkey and an alliance of Bulgaria, Serbia, Montenegro and Greece.
- Woodrow Wilson is elected as US President.
- Royal Flying Corps is established.
- Robert Scott reaches the South Pole.
- *Titanic* sinks off the coast of Newfoundland on its maiden voyage with the loss of 1,500 lives.
- Remains of Piltdown Man discovered; later found to be a hoax.
- The first Royal Variety Performance is held.
- The Ulster Covenant is signed against Home Rule.

The *Titanic* left Belfast on 2nd April, with Thomas Andrews on board, bound for Southampton.

On 9th April a great Unionist demonstration was held at Balmoral, addressed among others by Andrew Bonar Law, leader of the Conservative and Unionist Party. The previous day, Comber Square had been the venue for a similar event, albeit on a smaller scale:

Andrew Bonar Law at Balmoral 9th April 1912

Mr Bonar Law had a splendid reception at Comber on Monday. The whole of the townspeople and the inhabitants of the surrounding countryside seemed to have been attracted as by an all-powerful magnet to The Square. Men, women and children united in giving the Unionist leader a stirring welcome. Almost every house in the town was bedecked with flags, and everywhere the Union Jack, fluttering in the gale of wind, met the eye. In the centre of The Square, under the shadow of the fine monument to the memory of General Gillespie, a platform had been erected to accommodate the distinguished visitors and the leading residents of the district ... Shortly after noon the members of the Orange Lodges of the district and of the Comber Unionist Club marched from their headquarters, led by the band of the 2nd Comber Boys' Brigade, and formed a guard of honour. The band returned to the Belfast Road to await Mr Bonar Law's arrival ... It was past one o'clock when the motor from Belfast conveying the Unionist leaders was sighted, and immediately there was a prolonged outburst of cheering. Hats and sticks and handkerchiefs were waved as the visitors, headed by the Boys' Brigade Band, approached the platform, and the cheering was renewed as the Right Hon. A Bonar Law, Lord Londonderry, Sir Edward Carson and the Right Hon. Walter Long mounted the platform ...

After speeches, the Unionist leaders proceeded on to Newtownards.

* * * *

But Comber was soon to be plunged into gloom, because on the night of 14th April the mighty ship *Titanic* had its encounter with the iceberg and sank. Around 1,500 souls perished, among them Thomas Andrews Junior of Comber, who had designed the ship. The town went into mourning.

In Comber itself:

The morning service in the Unitarian Church, in which the Andrews family are pillars, will long be remembered, its memorial character being solemnised by the nearness of a common sorrow... Rev. Mr Dunkerley laboured under the stress of a deep emotion as he delivered his feeling tribute to the life and memory of the late Mr Thomas Andrews Jun.

At the close of the service, a resolution of sorrow and sympathy was passed in silence at a congregational meeting.

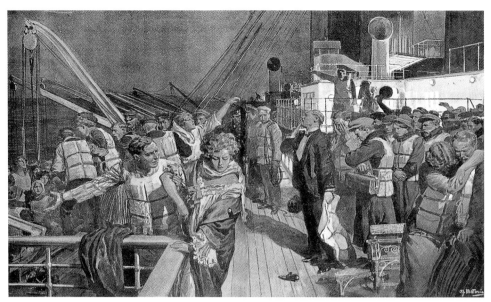

A Night to Remember

Such was the esteem in which Thomas was held by the people of Comber that his death had to be marked in some way.

> ... a meeting of the principal inhabitants of the town and neighbourhood was convened by circular... after due consideration it was unanimously resolved that the memorial should take the form of a Thomas Andrews Jun. Memorial Hall. A deputation was appointed to wait on the Andrews family at Ardara, and they heartily approved of the form the memorial was taking, and expressed their deep sense of gratitude to all who were interesting themselves in doing honour to their son's memory in his native town. Thus encouraged, the committee decided to take the general inhabitants into their confidence and convene a public meeting to approve of their actions and consider the question of finance. It has been decided that to build, equip and endow the hall a sum of £5,000 would be required. This, it was felt, was a considerable sum of money to raise, but the near relatives of the deceased, recognising the want of a public hall in Comber ... have promised liberal support to the undertaking.

John W. Ritchie was appointed as chairman of the committee in charge of building the hall. But before the end of the year he was dead, at the age of 58. Mr Ritchie was one of the town's foremost citizens, with a business in High Street:

> His commercial enterprise covered many branches of business, including that of grocer and provision dealer, wine and spirit merchant, newsagent, funeral undertaker, and general stores keeper ...

As managing-director of the Comber Gas Works, he proved himself to be a capable head of the company. The late Mr Ritchie was also secretary to the Comber Cemetery Committee ...

Island Hill had an unexpected visitor:

A number of yachtsmen, who make Island Hill their mooring quarters, noticed that something unusual was the matter in the vicinity from shortly after noon. On returning in the evening to moor their yachts, they saw a moving object in the water, which was conjectured by some to be a boat overturned. On closer investigation, by one who was intent on seeing the supposed boat, the object proved to be a whale, about 25 feet in length, and the fin of which, keeping above water, led to the deception. The intrepid investigator beat a hasty retreat, and in his efforts to row to a safe distance, almost capsized his own dinghy. The tide was ebbing rapidly, and from the frantic efforts made by the whale to get to deep water again, it was evident that it had been almost stranded. Having succeeded in its object in gaining deep water, the whale was soon lost to sight.

Ulster Day (28th September) was a momentous day throughout the Province. Comber was no exception:

... A special united service was held in the First Presbyterian Church at 2.30pm, when the church was filled, seats having to be provided in the aisles, all the clergymen taking part... After the service, men and women signed the Covenant and Declaration in large numbers in the church grounds, the Square, Mill Reading Room, and the Orange Hall, the utmost enthusiasm prevailing.

Sir Edward Carson signs the Covenant in Belfast City Hall

(MEN) 2324 SHEET No. 9

PARLIAMENTARY DIVISION. North Down
DISTRICT. Comber
PLACE OF SIGNING. Orange Hall

Covenant :—

BEING CONVINCED in our consciences that Home Rule would be disastrous to the material well being of Ulster as well as of the whole of Ireland, subversive of our civil and religious freedom, destructive of our citizenship, and perilous to the unity of the Empire, we, whose names are underwritten, men of Ulster, loyal subjects of His Gracious Majesty King George V., humbly relying on the God whom our fathers in days of stress and trial confidently trusted, do hereby pledge ourselves in solemn Covenant, throughout this our time of threatened calamity, to stand by one another in defending, for ourselves and our children, our cherished position of equal citizenship in the United Kingdom, and in using all means which may be found necessary to defeat the present conspiracy to set up a Home Rule Parliament in Ireland. And in the event of such a Parliament being forced upon us, we further solemnly and mutually pledge ourselves to refuse to recognise its authority. In sure confidence that God will defend the right, we hereto subscribe our names.

And further, we individually declare that we have not already signed this Covenant.

NAME.	ADDRESS.
Alexander Bennett	Comber
John Scott	Comber
David Crawford	Comber
Robert Jamie	Comber
Robert Robinson	Comber
William Mitchell	Comber
James Brown	Ballyaltikilligan Com.
Thomas Andrews	Ardara, Comber
Samuel Galbraith	Brownlow St Comber
Robert Donnan	2 Railway St Comber

Signatories of the Covenant in Comber Orange Hall

8

Postscript

> The first sod was cut on the 2nd October 1913 by Elizabeth Law Barbour Andrews, daughter of the late Thomas Andrews Jun, shipbuilder.

So reads an inscription on the Andrews Hall in Comber. Thomas' daughter was not quite three years old at the time. She was affectionately known as Elba, from the initials of her name. Elba never married and spent much of her life in Kenya. She loved driving, and owned a number of unusual cars. Unfortunately she was tragically killed in a road accident on 1st November 1973 when returning from visiting friends in Dublin. Her ashes were placed in the Andrews Mausoleum at St Mary's Parish Church.

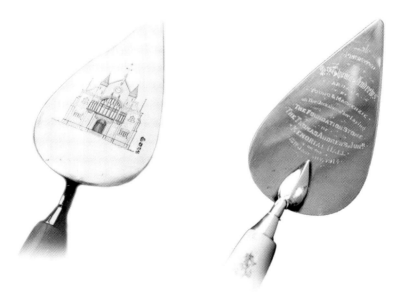

Trowel used to lay foundation stone of
Andrews Memorial Hall 13th January 1914

Eliza (Pirrie) Andrews 1845–1929

Another inscription records the laying of the foundation stone:

This stone was laid on the 13th January 1914 by Mrs Andrews, Ardara, Comber, mother of the late Thomas Andrews Jun, shipbuilder.

Thomas' mother, the former Eliza Pirrie, sister of Lord Pirrie, head of Harland and Wolff, continued to live at Ardara until her death on 10th March 1929 at the age of 84. Her husband, Thomas of Ardara, passed away on 17th September 1916, aged 73. His had been a distinguished career. For, as well as making a success of the mill, Thomas became President of the Ulster Liberal Unionist Association in 1892. This organisation was composed of Liberals opposed to Home Rule, and Thomas was heavily involved in organising the Ulster Convention of 1892. He was also Chairman of the Belfast and County Down Railway, Chairman of Down County Council and in 1912 High Sheriff of County Down.

Both Thomas and Eliza are buried in the family grave at Comber Non-Subscribing Church. And both are commemorated in stained glass windows there:

Erected by the members of this congregation in affectionate and grateful memory of their late fellow-member, the Right Hon. Thomas Andrews D.L. who died 17th September 1916.

So reads the inscription on the window in memory of Thomas, unveiled on 23rd December 1923 by Miss Mary Niblock, a member of the congregation. The upper portion bears figures representing Courage and Humanity, while the lower window is a representation of the Angel of Peace receiving a sword from a kneeling warrior, with rival armies in the background, and beyond them the rising sun. In the sky are depicted the dove and the olive branch, which formed the crest of the late gentleman.

Window entitled 'Peace' in memory of Thomas Andrews of Ardara

To the glory of God and in loving memory of Eliza Andrews, née Pirrie, who died on the 10th March 1929, wife of the Rt. Hon. Thomas Andrews D.L. Erected by their sixth child Mr William Andrews MBE, D.L.

The window in memory of Eliza was donated by her youngest son Willie and dedicated on 19th May 1963. There is much of interest in it, not least the depiction of a cricket bat and ball, drawing attention to Willie's lifelong enthusiasm for the sport.

Window entitled 'Love' in memory of Eliza Andrews

The window is entitled 'Love' and depicts a mother with six children, and a house in the background. That house is Ardara, the family home of Thomas and his wife Eliza, the woman is Eliza herself. The child she carries in her arms is the baby who died in January 1884 at about three weeks old. The other children are gathered around her, and so we are given a beautiful illustration of a mother's love for her children. What was the story of those children?

John Miller Andrews (right foreground) at cabinet meeting

The eldest son was John Miller Andrews, born 17th July 1871. He was one of Northern Ireland's foremost politicians, becoming Minister of Labour in the first Northern Ireland cabinet of 1921. He retained this portfolio until 1937 when he transferred to the Ministry of Finance. Then in 1940, at the grand old age of 69, he received the highest accolade of all, becoming Prime Minister in succession to Sir James Craig (Lord Craigavon). He led the Province through much of the turbulent Second World War period, until 1943 when he was replaced by Sir Basil Brooke. John Miller Andrews would remain an MP at Stormont until 1953. He died on 5th August 1956 and is buried in the family grave at Comber Non-Subscribing Church. On 10th September 1902 John Miller Andrews married Jessie Ormrod from Heaton near Bolton. Thomas Junior was best man.

Thomas was the second son, born 7th February 1873. As we have seen, his was a life spent in the shipbuilding trade, rising to become Managing Director of Harland and Wolff in Belfast, and losing his life on the *Titanic* on that fateful night of 14th–15th April 1912. He was only 39 years old.

Eliza Montgomery Andrews (known as Nina) was the only daughter, born 21st June 1874. On

Eliza Montgomery (Nina) Andrews 1874–1930

James Andrews 1877–1951,
from 1937 Lord Chief Justice of NI

Willie Andrews 1886–1966

26th April 1906 she married an Englishman, Lawrence Arthur Hind, in an impressive wedding ceremony at Comber Non-Subscribing Church. They lived in England and had three daughters, but in 1916 tragedy struck when Lieut-Col. Hind was killed at the Battle of the Somme. Nina returned to Ardara, and died on 30th June 1930, aged only 56.

The third son, James Andrews, born 3rd January 1877, had a distinguished career in the legal profession, rising to become Lord Chief Justice of Northern Ireland in November 1937. His wife was Jane or Jeannie Ormrod whom he married on 17th May 1922, a sister of Jessie, wife of John Miller Andrews. So we have two brothers marrying two sisters. James was knighted on 6th July 1942, the first of the family to receive that honour. He died on 18th February 1951.

William (Willie) was born on 25th August 1886. Along with John Miller Andrews, he was a director in the Comber Flax Spinning Mill of John Andrews & Co Ltd. Indeed, with his eldest brother so heavily involved in the affairs of the nation, it was left to Willie to hold the fort. Willie also served in the forces during both World Wars, reaching the rank of Captain. But his chief claim to fame was on the cricketing field, captaining North Down for many years, and making the odd appearance for Ulster and Ireland. He was also heavily involved in the administration of Ulster cricket. He died, unmarried, on 22nd December 1966.

What happened to the widow of Thomas Andrews Junior, Helen or Nellie as she was known? Well, Nellie remarried in 1917. Her second husband was Henry Harland, by whom she had three daughters and a son. They lived in London, where Henry worked in the offices of Harland and Wolff. After his death in 1945 she returned to Ireland to live at Dunmurry, dying in August 1966 at the age of 84. She is buried in the Barbour family tomb at Lambeg Parish Church.

One of the most poignant events in Nellie's life must have been the occasion of the opening of the Andrews Hall in Comber in memory of her late husband Thomas. This took place in 1915:

> This hall, which has been erected in Comber by the inhabitants of the town and district and other friends, was opened by Mrs Thomas Andrews jun., on the afternoon of Friday 29th January. At the request of the family, owing to the war and other circumstances, the ceremony was informal and private. The key was presented to Mrs Andrews by Mr Mackenzie of Messrs Young and Mackenzie, the architects of the hall. Mrs Andrews, in declaring the hall open, said – "Friends, in opening this Memorial Hall I would like to take advantage of the opportunity to express my very heartiest thanks to all the contributors for their great generosity, which is most deeply appreciated by me. Also, I wish to convey my warmest gratitude to the trustees and

Memorial Hall on Ballygowan Road

members of committee for the keen interest they have taken in all matters connected with the erection of this magnificent hall; and also the architects and builders for the time and thought they have so wholeheartedly devoted to the work. I hope this Memorial Hall will be a great benefit to the people of Comber, and I wish to add that it was very gratifying to me to be asked to open it.

The hall, which reflects great credit upon the builders (Messrs Courtney Bros) is built of handsomely-dressed stone, and is probably the finest building of its kind situated in any provincial town in Ireland. On the ground floor there are club rooms, consisting of billiard room, reading room, minor hall, committee room, kitchen etc., and above these rooms is the main hall, which will comfortably seat about 700 people. The intention is that the grounds which surround the hall will be laid out as a public park, which we are confident will be much appreciated by the people of the neighbourhood.

The grave of Thomas of Ardara and family

The Thomas Andrews Junior (Shipbuilder) Memorial Hall – to give it its full title – still stands today, a fitting tribute to an exceptional man of his time. In 1973 the Andrews Memorial School was housed within the premises, and today it is still part of the school complex, although a modern school opened in 1979 beside it. The very name of this school also bears tribute to Thomas Andrews.

But there is another monument to his memory in Comber. Take a walk up to the Non-Subscribing graveyard and seek out the burial place of Thomas Andrews of Ardara and his family. You will find all the names there – Thomas of Ardara himself, his wife Eliza, his sons John Miller, James and Willie, daughter Nina, even the infant who died in 1884. And there is also Thomas Junior, even though he lies beneath the ocean waves. Let us end with his epitaph to be found on the headstone:

> In loving memory of their second son Thomas, born 7th February 1873, lost at sea in the foundering of the SS *Titanic* 15th April 1912. Pure, just, generous, affectionate and heroic. He gave his life that others might be saved.

That just says it all.

Inscription in memory of Thomas Andrews Junior

ANDREWS/PIRRIE

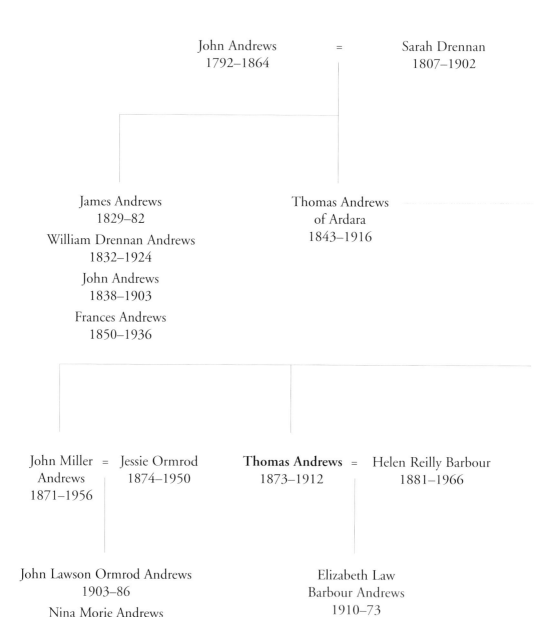

John Andrews
1792–1864 = Sarah Drennan
1807–1902

James Andrews
1829–82
William Drennan Andrews
1832–1924
John Andrews
1838–1903
Frances Andrews
1850–1936

Thomas Andrews
of Ardara
1843–1916

John Miller = Jessie Ormrod
Andrews   1874–1950
1871–1956

Thomas Andrews = Helen Reilly Barbour
1873–1912   1881–1966

John Lawson Ormrod Andrews
1903–86
Nina Morie Andrews
1904–81
Josephine Miller Andrews
1909–91

Elizabeth Law
Barbour Andrews
1910–73

FAMILY TREE

James Alexander Pirrie = Eliza Montgomery
1821–49   1820–95

Eliza Pirrie   William James Pirrie
1845–1929   1847–1924

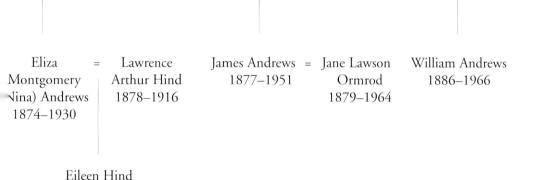

Eliza   =   Lawrence   James Andrews = Jane Lawson   William Andrews
Montgomery   Arthur Hind   1877–1951   Ormrod   1886–1966
Nina) Andrews   1878–1916   1879–1964
1874–1930

Eileen Hind
1907–93
Edith Hind
1909–97
Doreen Hind
1912–2002

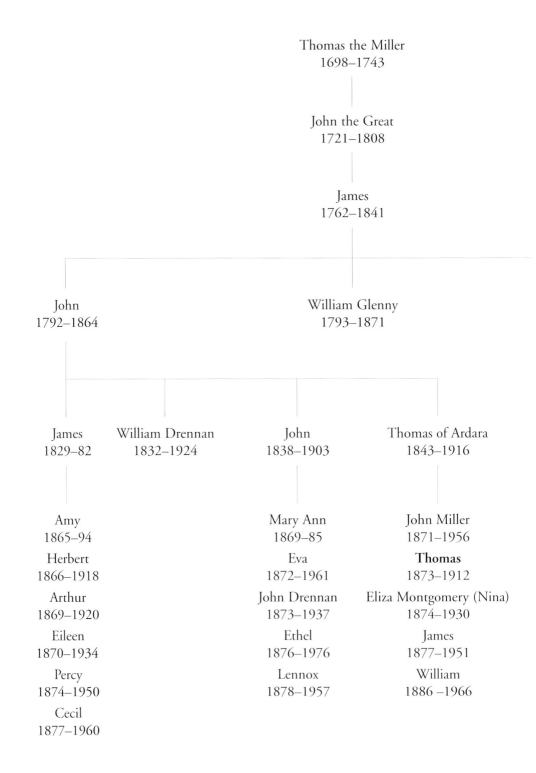

Thomas the Miller
1698–1743

John the Great
1721–1808

James
1762–1841

John
1792–1864

William Glenny
1793–1871

James
1829–82

William Drennan
1832–1924

John
1838–1903

Thomas of Ardara
1843–1916

Amy
1865–94

Herbert
1866–1918

Arthur
1869–1920

Eileen
1870–1934

Percy
1874–1950

Cecil
1877–1960

Mary Ann
1869–85

Eva
1872–1961

John Drennan
1873–1937

Ethel
1876–1976

Lennox
1878–1957

John Miller
1871–1956

Thomas
1873–1912

Eliza Montgomery (Nina)
1874–1930

James
1877–1951

William
1886 –1966

ANDREWS
FAMILY TREE
(SIMPLIFIED)

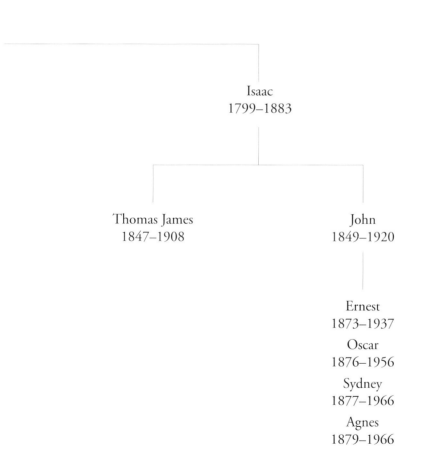

Isaac
1799–1883

Thomas James
1847–1908

John
1849–1920

Ernest
1873–1937

Oscar
1876–1956

Sydney
1877–1966

Agnes
1879–1966

Appendix 1

Address by Rev. Thomas Dunkerley to the congregation of Comber
Non-Subscribing Presbyterian Church on Sunday 21st April 1912

> Greater love hath no man than this, that a man lay down his life for
> his friend.
>
> JOHN 15:13

We meet this morning with hearts distressed by sorrow for the appalling disaster
which has filled so many homes with woe. The largest ship in the world,
magnificently appointed, elaborately planned, has gone down with its heavy
freight of human life. And from Royalty downwards the people of this great
Empire have been moved to serious grief. In the widely-felt suffering and sorrow,
no congregation has a deeper share than our own. One familiarly known to us all
– known from childhood upwards – has nobly, heroically, gone down in the ill-
fated vessel. Thomas Andrews Junior, member of the family held in such high
regard among us, has suddenly, but grandly, ended a career of the brightest
promise. You will bear with me as I mention a little personal matter. The "call"
which brought me to be your minister contained two or three signatures
evidently made by youthful penmen.

One of these, as I remember now with melancholy interest, was that of our lost
friend. The intimacy then begun grew and developed into tender and affectionate
friendship. I name this little fact, which has its interest for me, because I know it
is but an example of personal reminiscences which many of you cherish. His
kindly nature was such that each and all of you can recall some token of his genial
personality. We think of little incidents in his life as a boy in our midst, incidents
that prefigured the man that was to be. Among the contributions to the bazaar
which helped you to erect the adjoining schoolroom in the year 1879 were a
number of young kittens. One of these, having escaped, in its fright took refuge
in a place inaccessible to bigger creatures, and the prolonged efforts of many
helpers failed to induce it to come forth. But our friend, then a small schoolboy,
learning what had happened, called the timid pussy, and very soon it responded,
and forgetting its fears ran to what it recognised as amicable arms. The natural
instinct of the tiny pet told it where trust might be placed. The young schoolboy,
of course, was not deprived of his protégé, but becoming its owner proved a
tenderly indulgent master of what had so confidently committed itself to him. A

trifling incident! But character is manifested in such trifles. We see there the indication of the tender, manly heart that distinguished our lamented friend through life. Strength and mercy were combined in his truly religious nature.

He exemplified the words of the poet Coleridge:

> He prayeth best who loveth best
> All things both great and small;
> For the dear God who loveth us
> He made and loveth all.

We remember this day how our lost friend warmly shared the devotion of his family to our house of prayer and this congregation. We recall the presence with us of the two brothers, who in their youthful days were inseparable companions. So little was the difference in age and size that they seemed like twins, sharing every juvenile companion. The demands of business in later years and the establishment of separate homes could not impair the beautiful amity. Together the two brothers passed through my class for young communicants, and even after his new and happy home was formed in Belfast, 'Tommie' would elect to join us in our simple communion service. When the time came for a vocation in life to be decided on, our young friend's choice had long been formed, and he threw himself with all his native ardour into the pursuit of proficiency as a shipbuilding engineer. In the firm of Harland and Wolff he was closely associated with his uncle Lord Pirrie.

The young man, intelligent, industrious, earnest, enterprising and diligent to the point of strenuousness, reading while others played, through sheer toil and ability made for himself a position that few of his years attain – an authority in the construction of large vessels, and gave brilliant promise of higher things to come. But the promises were not destined to be realised. The end has come, an untimely one, as it seems to us. The building of the Titanic was his crowning work, and he had legitimate pride in showing his intimate friends over that triumph of modern engineering skill before it left Belfast. How little did they imagine that it so soon would be his tomb. His connection with his work was not that of a hireling. He had the true artistic spirit. His work must be good and true. It must satisfy his own exacting conscience. Only honest performance can come from high character. A man's work proclaims what he is. When the news came that the vessel was wrecked and that lives were lost, I knew and said that our friend was lost also; for it was not in him to save his own life at the cost of another's. All accounts tell of his heroism and his strenuous exertions to save others.

A cousin of his mother, Mr James Montgomery of New York, boarded the *Carpathia* on its arrival with the rescued in dock there and interviewed the surviving officers and passengers in regard to our friend. He cabled to the weeping mother – 'All unanimous, Andrews heroic unto death. Thinking only safety of others'.

A son is unspeakably dear to a parent. Yet a mother wrote to Mrs Andrews – 'I would be a proud and thankful woman if, when the day arrives for my son to face the portals of this life, I might have the joy of feeling he left behind him the unstained, noble record of your dear son'. I, as a parent, echo that wish. Less than four years ago our friend was married. It was one of the ideal unions sanctioned by perfect love. His young and gentle widow, who has one sweet infant, mourns this day her irreparable loss, and our sympathy flows forth to her and our earnest prayer rises to God that He who cares for the widow and the fatherless will support her and hers in this profound affliction. This morning our thoughts turn naturally and especially to the members of his bereaved home in our midst, whose empty seats speak to us of their suffering. We think of and sympathise with their profound sorrow. We think of the brother to whom I have referred, of the sister and brothers to whom the departed was inexpressibly dear, and of the honoured parents, whose autumn of life is thus overcast.

Who can minister consolation to them but God alone? We then, simply commend them to the All-Parent, whose love surpasses all human affection. The public prints have spoken of our friend as heroic. It is the true word to apply to his conduct. The hero may walk unrecognised by our side until the supreme stroke comes that parts us. But it is well for us to have known such. It is not the soldier alone who is the true hero.

> But dream not helm and harness
> The sign of valour true.
> Peace hath higher tests of manhood
> Than battle ever knew.
> Walking his round of duty
> Serenely, day by day,
> With the strong man's hand of labour,
> And childhood's heart of play.
> True as the knights of story,
> Sir Lancelot and his peers,
> Brave in his calm endurance
> As they in their tilt of spears.
> Knight of a better era
> Without reproach or fear,
> Said I not well that Bayards
> And Sydneys still are here.

Thomas Andrews has gone before us. The spirit within him that used to talk to us, to look at us with kind eyes, is no longer visible. But our prayer is – blessings on his memory. And it may be that he, beholding us, blesses us.

Appendix 2

Poem on Robert Rollo Gillespie by Sir Henry Newbolt

GILLESPIE

Riding at dawn, riding alone,
Gillespie left the town behind;
Before he turned by the Westward road
A horseman crossed him, staggering blind.

'The Devil's abroad in false Vellore,
The Devil that stabs by night,' he said,
'Women and children, rank and file,
Dying and dead, dying and dead.'

Without a word, without a groan,
Sudden and swift Gillespie turned,
The blood roared in his ears like fire,
Like fire the road beneath him burned.

He thundered back to Arcot gate,
He thundered up through Arcot town,
Before he thought a second thought
In the barrack yard he lighted down.

'Trumpeter, sound for the Light Dragoons,
Sound to saddle and spur,' he said;
'He that is ready may ride with me,
And he that can may ride ahead.'

Fierce and fain, fierce and fain,
Behind him went the troopers grim,
They rode as ride the Light Dragoons
But never a man could ride with him.

Their rowels ripped their horses' sides,
Their hearts were red with a deeper goad,
But ever alone before them all
Gillespie rode, Gillespie rode.

Alone he came to false Vellore,
The walls were lined, the gates were barred;
Alone he walked where the bullets bit,
And called above to the Sergeant's Guard.

'Sergeant, Sergeant, over the gate,
Where are your officers all?' he said;
Heavily came the Sergeant's voice,
'There are two living and forty dead'.

'A rope, a rope,' Gillespie cried:
They bound their belts to serve his need;
There was not a rebel behind the wall
But laid his barrel and drew his bead.

There was not a rebel among them all
But pulled his trigger and cursed his aim,
For lightly swung and rightly swung
Over the gate Gillespie came.

He dressed the line, he led the charge,
They swept the wall like a stream in spate,
And roaring over the roar they heard
The galloper guns that burst the gate.

Fierce and fain, fierce and fain,
The troopers rode the reeking flight:
The very stones remember still
The end of them that stab by night.

They've kept the tale a hundred years,
They'll keep the tale a hundred more:
Riding at dawn, riding alone,
Gillespie came to false Vellore.

Appendix 3

Extract for Comber from **Belfast and Ulster Directory 1870**

Comber is a market town in County Down, fourteen miles from Downpatrick, seven E.S.E. from Belfast, situated on the road from Belfast to Downpatrick. There is a handsome Masonic monument to General Gillespie. The river Comber upon whose banks the town is situated, and from which its name is derived, runs into Strangford Lough on the East side of the parish, and the tide flows to within a short distance of the town. There are two extensive distilleries, corn-mills, hotels, a bleach-green and a spinning mill. The church is a small handsome building. There are places of worship for Presbyterians, Unitarians, and Wesleyan Methodists. The educational institutions are a school, founded by Viscountess Castlereagh in 1813; one under Erasmus Smith's Charity, and Congregational and National Schools. A National School is attached to the Second Presbyterian Church, called Smyth's National School. The market is held on Tuesday. Fairs – January 5th, April 5th, June 28th, and Oct 19th. Population, in 1861, 1,713.

Post-office, Downpatrick Street – Joseph Shean, postmaster. Letters from Dublin and all parts of the South of Ireland, also from England, arrive every morning at 2-15, and are despatched at 10.30am. Letters from Scotland, Belfast and all other parts of Ireland arrive at 8 in the morning; the Scotch letters are despatched at 5pm to be in time for the Scotch boats. Letters from Downpatrick and intermediate places arrive every morning at 9 and are despatched every afternoon at 2.35. The last mail despatched daily is at 7.35pm.

Constabulary Station, Mill St – **R. Parker**, constable.
Inland Revenue Officers – **John Garnett**, Bridge St; Wm. Gillen, Square; John Cockburn, Mill St; **Hector McKenzie**, Downpatrick St.

PLACES OF WORSHIP
Parish Church, Square – **Rev. Geo. Smith**, rector
Presbyterian Church and Manse, Downpatrick St – **Rev. John Rogers**
Presbyterian Church and Manse, High St – **Rev. James M. Killen**
Unitarian Church and Manse, Mill St – **Rev. John Orr**
Wesleyan Methodist Chapel, Bridge St – **Rev. W. Hoey**, Downpatrick St

PUBLIC INSTITUTIONS
Erasmus Smith's School, Square – **Owen Laveille**, teacher
Infant School, Downpatrick St – **Mrs Turner**, teacher

GENTRY, CLERGY, ETC
Allen, George, Unicarville
Andrews, Wm. G., Mill St
Andrews, Isaac, Square
Andrews, James
Andrews, John
Andrews, Thomas
Atkinson, James, Square
Birch, James, Ballybeen
Birch, Miss Mary, Bridge St
Boyd, William, Ballywilliam Flax Mills
Colville, James, Booten Cottage
Cowan, Andrew, Killynether
Fisher, James, Camperdown
Frame, James, surgeon, High Street
Haslett, Samuel, Maxwell's court
Killen, Rev. James, High St
Millar, John, distiller, Square
McCance, The Misses, Bridge St
McConnell, Mrs Eleanor, Mill St
Orr, David, Eden Cottage
Orr, James, The Booten
Orr, Rev. John, Mill St
Ritchie, Henry D., New Comber House
Rogers, Rev. John, The Manse
Simonton, John, Nursery Villa
Smith, Rev. George, Glebe House
Stone, Samuel
Whitla, John, Ballyhenry House

TRADERS, ETC
Allen, George, tanner, Square
Andrews, James & Sons, millers and linen merchants, Mill St
Andrews, John & Co, flaxspinners
Anderson, J., spirit dealer, High St
Boal, Messrs, grocers, Square
Bole, Bros, grocers and leather cutters, Square
Bowman, Hugh, saddler, High St

Boyd, Mrs, Bridge St
Buchanan, John, carpenter
Buchanan, Mrs. Alice, milliner, Mill St
Carse, Maria, grocer, Mill St
Chamberlain, Robt., supervisor, Inland Revenue, Square
Connery, Robert, flax buyer, Bridge St
Corbett, John, watchmaker, Mill St
Davidson, Samuel, draper, Square
Gibson, John, carpenter, Bridge St
Gibson, Thomas, saddler, Square
Gillan, Wm., inland revenue officer, Square
Halliday, Jane, grocer, High St
Hamilton, Miss, dressmaker, Bridge St
Heaney, Robert, grocer, Square
Jeffrey's Hotel, Square
Jeffrey, James, spirit dealer, Square
Jervis, George, spirit dealer, Main St
Kennedy, William, grocer, Downpatrick St
Lindsay, Robert & Co., sewed muslin manufacturers, Square; **Robert Withers**, agent
Lindsay, Wm. J., spirit dealer, Mill St
Long, Ann, grocer and sewing agent, Downpatrick St
Maginn, Margaret, dyer, Downpatrick St
Miller, Archibald, letter carrier
Miller, John, malster and distiller, Downpatrick St and Bridge St
Milling, James, hotel, Square
Morrow, Miss, dressmaker, Mill St
Munn, William, blacksmith
Murphy, William, spirit dealer and smith, Square
Murphy, William, spirit dealer, Square
McBriar, A., draper, Mill St
McCulloch, Robt., tailor, Bridge St
McDonald, Jas., posting establishment, Mill St

McDowell, Jane, milliner, Mill St

McDowell, John, sewing agent, Mill St

McKeag, William, carpenter, Square

McMoran, George, grocer, Mill St

Orram, John Smith, Bridge St

Patton, Robert, Railway Inn, Mill St

Rea, John, butcher, Bridge St

Riddle, H., High St

Riddle, James, Mill St

Ritchie, Henry D., grocer, spirit, hardware and seed merchant, High St

Robb, Gawn, tailor, Mill St

Robb, Susan, dressmaker, Mill St

Robb, Wm, wheelwright, Mill St

Robinson, James, Bridge St

Robinson, J., cabinetmaker, Bridge St

Shean, Joseph, woollendraper and haberdasher, Downpatrick St

Simpson, Robert, spirit dealer, Downpatrick St

Simpson, Robert, grain merchant, South St

Simonton, John, manager, Northern Bank branch, Square

Todd, M., Railway Tavern, grocer etc, Mill St

Waddle, Robert, shoemaker, Mill St

Wilson, David, grocer, Downpatrick St

Wilson, David, grain merchant, South St

Withers, Robert, grocer, Square

CONVEYANCES

Train carries mail; and a coach (from Killyleagh) calls at James Milling's every morning, Sunday excepted, at 8.30.

To Killyleagh – a coach (from Belfast) calls at Milling's hotel every afternoon, Sunday excepted, at 4.45.

Appendix 4

Extract for Comber from **Belfast and Ulster Directory 1912**

Comber is a market town in County Down, fourteen miles from Downpatrick, seven E.S.E. from Belfast, situated on the road from Belfast to Downpatrick. There is a large square, where fairs and markets are held, and in the centre of which stands a handsome Masonic monument, erected to the memory of General Gillespie. The River Comber, upon whose banks the town is situated, and from which its name is derived, runs into Strangford Lough, on the east side of the parish, and the tide flows to within a short distance of the town. There are two extensive distilleries, corn mills, hotels, a bleachgreen, a spinning mill, and stitching factory. The Church of Ireland is a neat little building. There are places of worship for Presbyterians, Unitarians, Methodists, and a Roman Catholic Chapel. The educational institutions are a school, founded by Viscountess Castlereagh in 1813, one under Erasmus Smith's Charity, and Congregational and National Schools. A National School is attached to the Second Presbyterian Church, called Smith's National School. There are two Masonic Halls and an Orange Hall. The North Down Cricket Club has been in existence for over half a century, and still maintains its old prestige. There are also hockey and football clubs. The market is held every Tuesday. Fairs – January 5th, April 5th, June 28th, and October 19th. The population in 1911 was 2,589.

Post-office, Mill Street – Miss Patterson, post-mistress. Letters from Dublin and all parts of the South of Ireland, also from England, arrive every afternoon at 2-15, and are despatched at 10.30am. Letters from Scotland, Belfast and all other parts of Ireland arrive at 8am; Scotch letters are despatched at 5pm to be in time for the Scotch boats. Letters from Downpatrick and intermediate places arrive every morning at 9 and are despatched every afternoon at 2.35. The last mail despatched daily at 7.35pm.

The County Down Railway carries the mail, and Frank Morrow (from Killyleagh) calls at the Post Office every morning (Sundays excepted) at 9. Mail car from Ballydrain twice daily.

Constabulary Station, Mill Street [modern-day Castle Street] – **Sergeant P. Dinsmore**; Constables: **Patrick Fitzpatrick**, **Wilson R. Singleton**, **W. H. Irvine** and **M. Finerty**.

Inland Revenue Officers – **R.H. Collins**, supervisor; **James Walsh**, **Pierce Smiddy**, **S. McCully** and **W.G. Fegan**; Probate Officer, **James A. Beatty**; residence, Osmaston.

Comber Traders' Association – President, **John W. Ritchie**; vice-president, **William John Macdonald**; **John A. Macdonald**, treasurer and secretary.

PLACES OF WORSHIP
Parish Church, Square – **Rev. C.C. Manning**, Stormount, Laurel
    Bank, rector.
First Presbyterian Church, High Street – **Rev. Dr Graham**.
Salvation Army Hall, Mill Street – 3 and 7 pm.
Second Presbyterian Church and Manse, Killinchy Street – **Rev. Thomas McConnell**.
Wesleyan Methodist Chapel, Bridge Street – Various ministers each
    Sunday.
Unitarian Church and Manse, Mill Street – **Rev. Thomas Dunkerley**.

PUBLIC INSTITUTIONS
Erasmus Smith's School, Square.
Comber Gas Light Company Ltd – Chairman, **Right Hon. Thos. Andrews** PC, DL; managing director, **John W. Ritchie**; treasurer, **James F. Shean** JP; secretary, **John O. Abernethy**.

INHABITANTS
Robert Abernethy, Book-keeper
John Adair JP, Ballygraffin
James G. Allen JP, The Square
John Allen, The Square
Mrs Allen, Unicarville
The **Misses Anderson**, grocers, glass and
    china merchants, Mill Street
Herbert W. Andrews, The Old House
H.P. Andrews, Inla House
James Andrews BL, Ardara
Mrs Thomas J. Andrews, The Square
Mrs John Andrews, Uraghmore, Castle
    Street

John M. Andrews, Managing Director,
    Maxwell Court
John Andrews & Company Ltd,
    Flaxspinners
The Right Hon. Thomas Andrews DL,
    Chairman Belfast & County Down
    Railway Company, Ardara
William Andrews, Captain NDCC
    [North Down Cricket Club], Ardara
Joseph Berkeley, Nurseryville
Mrs William Berkeley, Nurseryville
Samuel Berkeley, Mount Alexander
Charles Blakiston-Houston, Deputy
    Master, North Down Harriers, The Ford

John Blair, Book-keeper, High Street
Mrs William Boyd, Ballywilliam
Samuel Brown, Miller, Maxwell Court Mill
George J. Bruce, Managing Director,
    Comber Distillery Company Ltd,
    Cuan, Carnesure
Hugh Busk, Cabinetmaker, Railway Street
James Cairns RDC [Rural District
    Councillor], Rosemount, Cherryvalley
Alexander Caughey, Secretary, Distilleries
James Park Cinnamond, Manager,
    Northern Bank Ltd, The Square
Edward Collins, Wholesale and retail
    grocer, tea, flour and provision
    dealer, and coal merchant, The Square
Miss Margaret Combe, Wistaston, Laurel
    Bank
James Corbitt, Brownlow Street
Hamilton Coulter, New Comber House
George P. Culverwell, Ashdene
Samuel Davidson, Draper, Castle Street
A.H. De Wind CE [Civil Engineer]
Samuel Drake, Draper, Mill Street
Alexander Dugan, Stonemason
John Dunn JP, Mossbank
Rev. Thomas Dunkerley, The Manse,
    Mill Street
Nathaniel Ferguson, The Moat
Frank Finlay, Engineer, High Street
James Fisher, Camperdown
Alfred Geddis, Tailor
John Gibson, Saddler, Bridge Street
Alex Glover, Posting Establishment, Mill
    Street
David Gold, Cashier, Northern Bank Ltd
J. Gordon, Grocer, Bridge Street
Rev. Dr Graham, The Manse, First
    Comber Presbyterian Congregation
W.T. Graham, Accountant, Glen View
Andrew Grainger, Gasfitter
John Gunning, Carpenter, Brownlow Street
David Hamilton, Trench House
Joseph Hedley, Gasworks, Mill Street
Dr Robert Henry, Dispensary Doctor,
    Registrar of Births and Deaths

Robert Henry MD, High Street
William Henderson, Cullintra House
John Herron, Ballyhenry
Mrs Thomas Herron, Ringcreevy
Thomas Herron, Ringcreevy
J. Hunter, Mill Manager, Londonderry
    Avenue
Thomas Huxley, Flax Mills, Joseph's
    Bridge
John Kane, Blacksmith
Miss Kennedy, Grocer, Killinchy Street
Matthew Kerr RDC [Rural District
    Councillor], Printer, Stationer,
    Bookseller and Publican, Bridge Street
    and The Square
Hugh Lindsay, Ballyhenry
Miss Long, High Street
M. Maginn, Dressmaker, Killinchy Street
Mrs Marshall, Refreshment Rooms
Kenneth Mawhinney, Island Hill
James Millen, Schoolmaster, High Street
R. & J. Milling, Grocers, publicans,
    timber and iron yard and
    weighmasters
Samuel Moore, Island Hill
David Munn, Cattogs House
James Munn, High Street
Matthew Munn, Carpenter
Miss Murdock, Crescent
W.J. Murdoch, The Crescent
John Murray, Schoolmaster, Railway Street
James McAlpine, Castleavery
Mrs David McAlpine, Mount Alexander
William McBride, Ivanhoe, Laurel Bank
Hugh McBurney, The Cottage and 73
    High Street, Belfast
Thomas McBurney, The Moat
Robert McBurney, Steam thresher
    proprietor, Ballyhenry
James McCracken, Longlands
The Misses McCracken, Ballyrickard
R. McCulloch, Bridge Street
A. McDonald, Posting Establishment,
    Mill Street
John A. McDonald, Grocer and posting

Wm. John McDonald, Grocer, Mill Street
Robert McDowell, Cherryvalley House
J. McIlvene, Shoemaker, Mill Street
John McKeag, Bootmaker, Mill Street
S.B. McKeag, Wholesale grocer, The Square
Messrs McKee, The Hill, Drumhirk
Robert McMillen, Spirit Dealer, Mill Street
James McMorran, Horse dealer, Alexandra House
Hugh McMorran, Castleavery
John McMorran, Bootmaker, Killinchy Street
James McRae, Schoolmaster
Francis McRoberts, VS [Veterinary Surgeon], The Square
Thomas McRoberts, Clothes dealer and draper
William McRoberts, Auctioneer, Mill Street
J. McWhinney, Butcher
David Nesbitt, Grocer, Mill Street
Mary Niblock, Grocer and spirit dealer, Bridge Street
William Niblock, Druggist, The Square
James Niblock, Hardware and general merchant and cycle agent, Castle Street
Andrew Oliver, Cutter and tailor, Mill Street
Alex Orr RDC [Rural District Councillor], Ballystockart
Blakely Orr & Sons, Knocknasham Mills
Mrs Osborne, Glenview
Thomas Patton, Railway Inn, Mill Street
Paisley & Co, Drapers, millinery, boot and shoe warehouse, Mill Street and Crossroads, Killinchy
William Pinnance, Tailor, draper, outfitter etc, Castle Street
John Proctor, Distillery Manager
John Quinn, Stonemason, Mill Street
Mrs Hugh Reid, Bridge Street
John Ritchie, Mill View, Cullintra
Miss Riddle, High Street

Mrs Ritchie, Cullintra
John W. Ritchie, Wine, spirit, coal, timber and iron merchant, funeral undertaker and family grocer. Agent for *Belfast News-Letter* and *Belfast Weekly News*
John Robinson, The Flow, Cattogs
S.P. Robinson, General Draper, the Noted House for boots and shoes, hosiery, corsets, ladies' and children's underclothing, men's, youths' and boys' ready-made suits, Castle Street
Russell & Niblock, Insurance agents, Castle Street
George M. Shaw, Manufacturer, Carnesure
Mrs William Shaw, Cattogs
James Shean JP, Killinchy Street
Alexander Shields, Bridge Street
A. Simpson, Grain merchant and spirit dealer
James Simpson, Book-keeper, Killinchy Street
James Skillen, Blacksmith, Mill Street
James Smith, Butcher, Mill Street
George Sowerby, Book-keeper, The Crescent
George Spence, Clerk, Brownlow Street
William Spence, Schoolmaster, Railway Street
Dr Robert Steele, The Square
Richard Stevenson, Bridge Street
Miss Stone, Barnhill
Samuel Stone JP, Barnhill
Hugh Strickland, Butcher
John Thompson, Tailor, Mill Street
Hugh David Todd, Railway Tavern, Mill Street
William Todd, High Street
Dr Wallace, Lisbarnett
Hamilton Watt, Carpenter, Mill Street
R.J. White, Fancy goods dealer, Mill Street
J. Wightman, Shoemaker, High Street
Mrs R. Withers, Grocer, The Square

Appendix 5

Comber Historical Society

Comber Historical Society was formed in 2000 and aims to promote and preserve the rich history and heritage of the town and district. Guest speakers attend on the second Monday of each month between September and April and speak on a variety of topics. Over the years, the colourful and eclectic programme has ranged from the old monastic settlement at Nendrum to the building of the Comber bypass; from Comber in the 1830s to the Belfast and County Down Railway; from the Ards Tourist Trophy (TT) Race to Saint Patrick; and from the history of North Down Cricket Club to Comber's *Titanic* connections.

In addition to these monthly meetings, the Society organises summer outings to historic places such as Carrickfergus, Greyabbey, Belfast's Titanic Quarter and Belfast City Hall. C.H.S. also arranges conducted tours of Comber, including the Thomas Andrews Trail.

Over the years, Comber Historical Society has been associated with a number of key projects:

Society Committee Members, Len Ball and Desmond Rainey produced an excellent book on the history of the town. *A Taste of Old Comber* gives a nod to the town's whiskey-distilling past – and provides a comprehensive overview of Comber's history.

The late Norman Nevin MBE was an enthusiastic local historian. In 2009, Comber Historical Society marked the centenary of his birth with a series of events, including an exhibition in Comber Library, a themed walking tour, and talks to the local schools.

The Society now has a presence on the internet at **www.comberhistory.com**. A wealth of local information is supplemented by downloadable PDFs of two key documents: Norman Nevin's *History of Comber*; and Jim Gracey's *Historical Directory of People and Places in Comber*. C.H.S. is proud to be the custodian of these important pieces of research. The website also allows people to post queries and comments relating to Comber's history.

'The Abbey Stones' are a gift to the town of Comber from the Willis family – and the 19 original stones from Comber Abbey have now been permanently housed in St Mary's Parish Church where they feature as part of the St Patrick's Trail.

Comber Historical Society works closely with Ards Tourism to produce relevant tourist material including a downloadable app, walking guides, literature and town signage.

C.H.S. are currently involved with all things *Titanic*. To mark the centenary of the ship's launch in 2011, the Society worked with Andrews Memorial Primary School on a programme of events including an exhibition, a number of talks, and a nostalgic film show. Further events will take place next year to commemorate the tragic events of April 1912.

Index